Outstanding
Dissertations
in
Linguistics

edited by
Jorge Hankamer ■ Harvard University

A Garland Series

Subject and Object
in Modern English

Barbara Hall Partee

Garland Publishing, Inc. ▪ New York & London
1979

Library of Congress Cataloging in Publication Data

Partee, Barbara Hall.
   Subject and object in modern English.

   (Outstanding dissertations in linguistics)
   Originally presented as the author's thesis,
Massachusetts Institute of Technology, 1965.
   Bibliography: p.
   1. English language—Topic and comment. 2. English
language—Grammar, Generative. I. Title. II. Series.
PE1380.P3   1979   425   78-66576
ISBN 0-8240-9679-7

All volumes in this series are printed on acid-free,
250-year-life paper.
Printed in the United States of America

CONTENTS

CHAPTER III.   VERB AND OBJECT

ACKNOWLEDGEMENTS

My greatest debt is to Professor Noam Chomsky, whose contributions to both linguistic theory and English syntax are reflected (however inadequately) on every page, and who read and made valuable comments on the first draft of Chapters II and III. I am also deeply indebted to Professor Edward Klima for passing on to me some of his wealth of knowledge of and insights into the structure of English as well as his enthusiasm for the subject, and for also making critical comments on the first draft of Chapters II and III. I have benefited from discussions with Professor Paul Postal, T.M. Lightner, J.R. Ross, S.Y. Kuroda, and P.S. Rosenbaum.

I am grateful to the MITRE Corporation for providing an opportunity during the past two summers to work on English syntax and procedures for its analysis. I would like to give special thanks to Dr. Joyce Friedman of MITRE and Harvard University, who programmed the MITRE analysis procedure for transformational grammars, for her assistance in using it to check the transformations in Chapter III, as well as for encouragement and advice which if better heeded might have resulted in a thesis of higher quality and later completion.

I am also grateful to the Research Laboratory of Electronics of M.I.T. and the National Science Foundation for providing for my physical comfort.

LIST OF ILLUSTRATIONS

CHAPTER I

INTRODUCTION

1.1 Deep and Surface Sentence Structure

The aim of a syntactic study of a language is to discover the regu-
larities and generalizations underlying the sentence structure of that
language as one step in the process of explaining how the speaker of a
natural language is able to produce and understand a potentially infinite
set of sentences he has never produced or heard before. The transformational approach to syntax, first introduced by Zellig Harris[1] and
greatly expanded and enriched by Noam Chomsky[2], is based on the observation that most sentences are best described as the result of applying
various operations such as substitutions, deletions, and adjunctions to
one or more simpler sentences. The simple sentences are described by
phrase structure rules, or immediate constituent analysis, which were at
one time proposed as the best way to describe the entire structure of
all sentences; convincing arguments have been adduced to show that phrase

1. "Co-occurrence and transformation in linguistic structure",
    Language, 33, No. 3 (July-September 1957), 283-340. Reprinted in
    Jerry A. Fodor & Jerrold J. Katz, The Structure of Language:
    Readings in the Philosophy of Language (Englewood Cliffs: Prentice-
    Hall, Inc., 1964), pp. 155-210.

2. The Logical Structure of Linguistic Theory (Cambridge: mimeographed
    and microfilmed, M.I.T. Library, 1955)

    Syntactic Structures (The Hague: Mouton & Co., 1957). For addi-
    tional references, see the bibliography.

structure rules are not nearly as well suited for describing all of sentence structure as are a combination of phrase structure and transformational rules.[3]

The phrase structure component of the set of syntactic rules consists of an ordered set of context-sensitive rewriting rules of the form:

$$XAY \longrightarrow XZY$$

where A is a single non-terminal category symbol, and X, Y, and Z are arbitrary strings of terminal and non-terminal symbols, except that Z may not be null; application of the rule is the replacement of A by Z in a string which contains XAY as a substring. A derivation consists of writing down the designated initial symbol, usually chosen to be S, and then applying a subset of the rules in the order in which they are given in the grammar. The rules may introduce new occurrences of the symbol S; the whole set of rules is gone through again for each new occurrence of S.

After the phrase structure derivation has reached a point at which there are no non-terminal symbols left in the string, lexical items are substituted for the terminal category symbols. The phrase structure description of the sentence can be represented by a tree called a phrase-marker (P-marker) whose lowest nodes are the lexical items and whose branching points indicate replacement of one symbol by others in the derivation. The whole tree represents what can be called the

---

3.   Paul Postal, "Constituent Structure", _International Journal of American Linguistics_ (Bloomington: Publication Thirty of the Indiana University Research Center in Anthropology, Folklore, and Linguistics, 1964)

deep structure[4] of the sentence being derived; the deep structure contains all the information necessary for the semantic interpretation of the sentence[5], although the string of terminal symbols may be very different from that in the final form of the sentence.

The transformational component of the grammar consists of rules which map P-markers into other P-markers. A transformational rule has two parts:

(1) the structural description, which specifies a partition of a tree, and a set of conditions which the tree must meet; all and only those trees which can be partitioned in accordance with the structural description of a given transformation in such a way as to meet all the stated special conditions are in the domain of that transformation. Whether the transformation must be applied to a tree which is in its domain depends on whether the transformation is designated as optional or obligatory.

(2) the structural change, which specifies how a new tree is to be formed on the basis of the old tree. Technically, the structural change is effected by a set of elementary transformations; in this work the change is indicated in a common abbreviated notation.[6] One item of

4. Chomsky, "Current issues in linguistic theory", in Fodor and Katz, The Structure of Language, op. cit., p. 52.

5. Jerrold J. Katz and Paul M. Postal, An Integrated Theory of Linguistic Descriptions (Cambridge: The M.I.T. Press, 1964)

6. The notation used is essentially the same as that used in Noam Chomsky, "A transformational approach to syntax", in A.A. Hill (ed.), Proceedings of the Third Texas Conference on Problems of Linguistic Analysis in English, 1958 (Austin: The University of Texas, 1962) pp. 124-158. Reprinted in Fodor and Katz, The Structure of Language, op. cit., pp. 211-245.

notation used here which is not quite as universal as the rest is the use of the symbols "⟨" and "⟩" to mean "immediately dominates on the leftmost branch" and "immediately dominates on the rightmost branch" respectively. These symbols may be used as part of either the structural description or the designation of the structural change.

The ordering of transformations is not a completely settled issue; however, the only sort of ordering used here that is not widely agreed on is that of allowing a single transformation to apply over and over again in "the same place" (not identically the same each time, since the transformation changes the structure on each application so that eventually it may no longer apply). This cyclical ordering is used only for the transformation TOBJORD-1 in §3.331.

The P-marker which results after all the transformations that are going to be applied have been applied is a representation of what has been called the surface structure[7] of the sentence. The set of transformations taken all together then maps the deep structure of a given sentence onto its surface structure. It appears that the phonological rules operate on the surface structure to give the actual phonological shape of the sentence.[8]

1.2 Categories and Relations

The non-terminal symbols used in the phrase structure development of the base structure and in the structural descriptions of the transformations are all category symbols referring to phrase-types and word-

7. Chomsky, "Current issues in linguistic theory", p. 52.
8. Ibid., p. 54.

types that play a functional role in the grammar. There are also syntactic <u>relations</u> that are important in determining the semantic interpretation of sentences and cannot be ignored in explaining the similarity all speakers of a language feel to exist between sentences such as "That car is difficult to steer", "That car steers with difficulty", and "Mary steered that car with difficulty", or between active and passive sentences, or any of a number of other sorts of related sentences.

Grammatical relations can in many cases be given definitions of the form (X,Y), read "X of Y", where X is a category immediately dominated in the base structure by the category Y. For instance, since the subject of the sentence is the only noun phrase immediately dominated by the node S, the subject relation can be defined as (NP, S). In general, a definition of a relation (X,Y) is meaningful and non-vacuous as long as there are some trees in which Y directly dominates one and only one node labelled X. The definition is equally inapplicable whether there are too few or too many nodes labelled X dominated directly by a given Y.

1.3 Partial and Complete Grammars

As has been repeatedly emphasized in the literature connected with transformational grammars[9], it is not to be expected that any discovery procedure will be found for identifying the category or role in the grammar of any particular constituent short of constructing a complete grammar and testing it by comparing it overall with other grammars. A problem therefore arises when one tries to work on anything but a complete grammar, namely that contrasting hypotheses about a particular part of

9.   See, for instance, Chomsky, <u>Syntactic Structures</u>, p. 52

the grammar cannot really be tested. The problem with trying to write a complete grammar, on the other hand, is that a great many decisions must be made and justified in detail, and for each such detailed discussion the original problem of how to substantiate any claims in a small subsection of the grammar arises just as strongly as before.

One result of these difficulties is that syntactic arguments sometimes look circular, since the more complex and interwoven the rules are that are being discussed (and the larger a subset of the grammar one tries to deal with, the more interconnected the rules inevitably become), the more difficult it is to find any argument which can come first without demanding considerable tolerance from the reader with respect to claims that are made at the beginning but not justified until later.

1.4 Scope of the Thesis

The second chapter deals with subjects, first comparing two possible notions of derived subject and then re-examining some derived subjects which had been assumed to be underlying subjects as well, and concluding that in fact they are not.

The third chapter is concerned with the basic verb phrase relations; not only direct and indirect objects, but locative and directional phrases, with-phrases, and of-phrases are considered. Because of the problems mentioned above which arise in working on a small subset of English syntax, most of the conclusions reached are quite tentative.

CHAPTER II

THE SUBJECT RELATION

2.0 Introduction

Few grammarians have given much attention to defining the relation
"subject of a sentence",[1] for a number of reasons.

In the first place, the constituent generally recognized as subject
in the superficial structure can be identified in many cases by simple
formal criteria, such as word order, agreement with the verb, and for
some pronouns, case endings.

Secondly, although there is no simple way to make the formal criteria mentioned above into a concise necessary and sufficient condition
for subjecthood, this lack is not very strongly felt, since most grammarians agree on what is subject in any particular sentence; hence the
most common procedure is to give a few examples of subjects and proceed
from there, possibly offering a definition but seldom referring to it to
settle any questionable cases.

Thirdly, although various people have given some thought to trying
to identify the grammatical relation of subject with some notional re-

---

1. The locutions "subject of a sentence", "subject of a verb", and
simply "subject" will be used interchangeably, since no ambiguity
can arise; in all cases a relation, not a category, is being referred to.

lation such as actor or agent, it has always been easy to refute any
claimed identification of that sort by finding pairs of sentences which,
at least in their superficial structures, are grammatically similar but
notionally different or vice versa, e.g.:

(2-1, 2-2)   I like that. -- That pleases me.

(2-3, 2-4)   He suffered torture. -- He inflicted torture.

(2-5, 2-6)   He got his work done. -- He got his head cut off.

Otto Jespersen[2] discusses a number of attempts to find a logical or
psychological basis for the notion of subject and gives good arguments
against identifying most of the suggested notions with any grammatically
significant relation.[3] (However, he dismisses as equally useless, without any argument, Steinthal's claim that "in guter vater ist gut, logisch
betrachtet, eben so wohl prädicat zum subject vater, wie in der vater
ist gut,"[4] and the claim that the grammatical agent in a passive sentence is the logical subject, both of which can be given grammatical
significance by distinguishing deep from surface structure.) But
Jespersen himself offers a definition of subject which is virtually
empty:

2.   The Philosophy of Grammar [hereafter POG] (London: George Allen &
     Unwin Ltd., 1924), pp. 147-150.

3.   The following quotation from Hermann Paul, Principles of the History
     of Language, trans. H.A. Strong (London: Swan Sonnenschein, Lowrey,
     and Co., 1888), p. 314, illustrates the degree of discrepancy
     reached by some grammarians between the psychological or logical and
     grammatical notions of subject: "Every member of a sentence, in
     whatever grammatical form it may appear, is capable, from a psycho-
     logical point of view, of being subject, predicate, or copula, or a
     constituent of any of them."

4.   H. Steinthal, Charakteristik der Hauptsächl. Typen des Sprachbaues
     (Berlin, 1860), quoted in Jespersen, POG, p. 149.

"The subject is the primary which is most intimately connected
with the verb in the form which it actually has in the sentence
with which we are concerned; thus Tom is the subject in
(1) 'Tom beats John', but not in (2) 'John is beaten by Tom',
though both sentences indicate the same action on the part of
Tom; in the latter sentence John is the subject, because he is
the person most intimately connected with the verb beat in the
actual form employed: is beaten." [5]

This definition is immediately followed by a test for subjecthood whose

relation to the definition is not at all clear:

"We can thus find out the subject by asking Who (or What) followed
by the verb in the form used in the sentences: (1) Who beats
(John)? Tom. (2) Who is beaten (by Tom)? John." [6]

That Jespersen does not actually restrict his concept of subject to

that specified by his definition is clear from his recognition of an

underlying subject in subordinate constructions such as "judged me a

happy man", "elected Tom their chief", and "make the watch go." [7]

Chomsky has claimed[8] that in a transformational grammar it is pos-

sible to make a precise definition of the subject relation, and in fact

to distinguish at least two grammatically significant but distinct notions.

A relation can be defined in terms of a configuration of the base trees

as (NP, S), using the notation described in Chapter I. This is the re-

lation which has in the past often been called "logical subject", as in

the discussion above, but from the point of view of transformational

---

5. A Modern English Grammar on Historical Pinciples [hereafter MEG]
   (London: George Allen & Unwin Ltd., 1909-1949), III, 206.

6. Ibid, 207.

7. MEG, V, 8.

8. Aspects of the Theory of Syntax (Cambridge: M.I.T. Press,
   forthcoming).

grammar it might better be called "base subject" or "underlying subject". The relation which has generally been called "grammatical subject" clearly has to do with surface rather than base structure; hence in what follows, the terms "surface subject" or "derived subject" will be used in place of "grammatical subject" except when the views of earlier grammarians are being directly referred to. This latter notion has not been given a precise definition in transformational terms; one might suggest the following:

"The surface subject of a sentence is whichever constituent functions in the verb person-and-number agreement rule, if any."[9]

2.1 Surface Subject Defined by Number Agreement

The definition of surface subject is significantly different from that of underlying subject. In the base structure, there are a finite number of grammatical relations determined by the rules of the base component, and the only decision that needs to be made is which (if not all) of those relations are worth having names for. Outside of the base structure, however, the possible relations are not specified in the same way by the form of the rules, and one must essentially start from scratch to see, first of all, what relations (if any) outside the base structure should be defined, and then whether from these some general constraints on possible surface relations can be determined.

9. Note that neither the definition of underlying subject nor that of surface subject offers a procedure for deciding whether a particular constituent bears one of these relations to anything or not, short of constructing a grammar and looking at the derivation of the sentence in which the given constituent occurs. One task of linguistics is to find relations which play a functional role in the language, so it is natural that relations should be defined in terms of the rules of the language.

Since the notion of grammatical subject has been so universally accepted, it seems reasonable to consider it a likely first suggestion as to what should be a definable surface relation. Let us then first examine the consequences of the proposed definition.

(1) In the simple cases such as passive sentences and conjunction, the definition certainly agrees with what has always been called the grammatical subject.

(2) In the case of "anticipatory _it_", as in

(2-7) It surprises me that John knows about you.

the relative ordering of the agreement transformation and the transformation which moves the that-clause to the end of the sentence is not clear, since the verb would be made singular in either case. If reasons are found for ordering the postposing transformation first, then "it" is the surface subject according to the suggested definition. If the agreement transformation comes first, then "it that John knows about you" is the surface subject if the underlying structure is "it COMP", but if, as others have suggested, the underlying structure has just an abstract nominalization marker "NOM" or "COMP" and the "it" is not introduced until the postposing takes place, then just "that John knows about you" is the surface subject as well as the underlying subject. This last alternative seems to correspond to Jespersen's and Curme's ideas, since they both call "that John knows about you" the real subject of the sentence (where "real" means grammatical, not logical, in their usage) and "it" a "representative subject" [10] or "anticipatory subject".[11]

---

10. Jespersen, _MEG_, III, 25.

11. George O. Curme, _Syntax_, Vol. III of Hans Kurath and G.O. Curme, _A Grammar of the English Language_ (3 vols.; Boston: D.C. Heath & Co., 1931), p. 10.

- 18 -

Note that if one accepts this last conclusion, then the notion of surface
subject will not correspond to position in the surface tree even in
simple declarative sentences, as it will not in questions and inverted
sentences such as "Here comes the train."

(3) In the case of "anticipatory there", as in

(2-8) There is a spy in our midst.

(2-9) There are lions in that forest.,

"there" would not be considered the surface subject under the proposed
definition, since the number is determined by the noun.[12] This accords
with the descriptions of Curme[13] and Jespersen[14].

As for dialects in which "there is" (or rather, "there's") tends to
be used before singular and plural noun phrases alike, the suggested
definition would say that "there" is coming to be analyzed as the surface subject. As a native speaker of such a dialect, it seems wrong to
say that there is any such distinction between the two dialects; it
seems much more likely that the proposed definition is wrong and that
number agreement is peripheral rather than central to the notion of
surface subject. Or it may simply be that such dialects have a late
rule which converts both "there is" and "there are" to "there's". Let

---

12. Person agreement, which in general occurs between the verb and
     whichever element determines number agreement, appears to be
     absent in the case of anticipatory "there":

     There is only me left to do it.
     There is only you.
     There are only you three left in the competition.

13. Syntax, p. 10.

14. POG, p. 155.

us leave this question for the time being and continue examining the
consequences of the definition. (The interesting question of whether
such sentences with "be" as "My brother is the pitcher" and "The pitcher
is my brother" have the same underlying subject or not will not be considered here.)

(4) The situation with regard to imperatives is not quite clear.
Even if number agreement applies before the underlying "you" is deleted,
its effects are lost, since only the verb stem appears in the final
sentence ("be", not "are" or "were"). Hence there is no way to tell
whether the proposed definition would yield no surface subject or "you"
as surface subject until some basis is found for establishing a relative
ordering of the two rules. (If it should turn out that the two rules
are relatively unordered, as is conceivable, then the proposed definition
of surface subject would be shown to be ill-formed.)

(5) Jespersen points out that in the following sentences "we have
what should be logically a nexus expressed in the form of an adjunctal
group:"[15]

(2-10)   Too many cooks spoil the broth.

(2-11)   Many hands make light work.

(2-12)   No news is good news, isn't it?

What Jespersen does not point out is that there is some variation in the
use of singular and plural in such cases. The following sentences, for
instance, sound quite natural to some people:

15. MEG, III, 204.

(2-13)   Ten people in the car naturally makes it go slower.

(2-14)   No soldiers guarding the door bothers you, doesn't it?

The underlying subject in all these cases clearly contains a sentence; the deleted part is probably something like "there being". In this case the vacillation in ordering of the deletion and agreement rules (if that is what is really going on) does seem to have some relation to what is felt to be the surface subject, in that the presence of the deleted elements seems to be more strongly felt if the number agreement rule comes first and less strongly if the number agreement is determined solely by the remaining noun phrase.

The cases considered above do not provide conclusive evidence either for or against the suggested definition of surface subject. If more favorable evidence can be found, it might be suggested that agreement rules are one form of rule in terms of which surface relations can be defined. English does not provide much opportunity to explore such a hypothesis very far, however.

2.2 Surface Subject Defined by Substitution

An alternative definition of surface subject might be:

"The constituent in a surface tree which counts as its surface subject is whatever remains of the underlying subject if it has not been substituted for or else any constituent that has been substituted for the subject."

This definition requires that substitution transformations be clearly distinguished from permutations and adjunctions. It would have the following consequences in the cases discussed above.

(1) In the passive, the original object is substituted for the subject, so it will count as surface subject. In conjunction, the situation is rather complicated, but if this definition turns out to be a desirable one it will provide additional motivation for an analysis which treats all the conjoined sentences as exactly parallel, rather than arbitrarily treating the first one as special in adjoining the subjects of the following sentences to the subject of the first.

(2) Anticipatory "it" will necessarily be treated as surface subject whether it is considered as a part of the underlying subject or as transformationally introduced in its place.

(3) In the case of anticipatory "there", it is not clear that the "there" should be substituted for the subject. In a sentence such as

(2-15)   There are three cats on the roof.

there are several possible analyses. One possibility is that the underlying structure of (2-15) is the same as that of the simple sentence:

(2-16)   Three cats are on the roof.

Two different transformations can be thought of that would convert (2-16) into (2-15), which would have different consequences with respect to the question of whether "there" is the surface subject by the second definition.

(a) If "there" is substituted for the subject and the original subject moved to the right of "be", then "there" would be the surface subject.

(b) If, on the other hand, "there" plus the original AUX and "be" were all adjoined to the left of the original subject, "there" would not be considered the surface subject, but rather the underlying subject would also be the surface subject.

Of these two alternatives, (a) would be preferable, since "there" does act like the subject in a number of transformations:

(2-17)   For there to be so much time left bothers me.

(2-18)   There being so much time left bothers me.

(2-19)   There are three cats on the roof, aren't there?

However, neither of the above singularly transformations accounts for sentences such as the following:

(2-20)   There is a question I would like to ask you.

(2-21)   There is nothing for us to do.

(2-22)   There is someone to see you.

These sentences suggest that an embedding transformation is involved, since the sources which would be required for their derivation by either (a) or (b) above are missing:

(2-23)   *A question I would like to ask you is.

(2-24)   *Nothing for us to do. is.

(2-25)   *Nothing is for us to do.

(2-26)   *Someone to see you is.

(2-27)   (*) Someone is to see you.[16]

One possible form for the underlying structure involves an embedded S associated with "there"; for example, the underlying structure of (2-20) might be:

---

16. Although (2-27) is grammatical, it is not a paraphrase of (2-22).

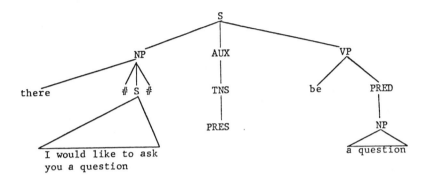

Fig. 2-i

The embedded sentence would be postposed, and an embedding transfor-

mation would delete the repeated element. It is not quite so clear how

(2-21) and (2-22) are to be derived, but presumably an embedding trans-

formation will also be required in those cases. With these derivations,

"there" is definitely regarded as the surface subject, since it is the

only remaining part of the underlying subject.

(4) Imperatives would clearly have no surface subject under this

definition; in fact, they do not.

(5) If we were to accept the second definition of surface subject

and abandon the first, then the previous discussion of the vacillation

in number after "too many cooks", etc., while still relevant to the

analysis of this phenomenon, would no longer be relevant to the determi-

nation of the surface subject. The nominal expressions would be the

surface subjects regardless of number, since they are the remnants of underlying subjects.

The discussion of the two definitions is summarized in the following
table:

TABLE I. SURFACE SUBJECT

	CONSTRUCTION	DEFINITION BY AGREEMENT RULE	DEFINITION BY SUBSTITUTION CONDITION
(1)	Passive subject	YES	YES
	Conjoined subjects	YES	?
(2)	IT	?	YES
(3)	THERE is/are	NO	YES
	THERE's	YES	YES
(4)	YOU in imperative	?	NO
(5)	TOO MANY COOKS spoil ...	YES	YES
	TOO MANY COOKS spoils ...	NO	YES

Although this discussion has been inconclusive, the table shows
that the second definition comes closer than the first to the traditional
notion of grammatical subject. Furthermore, the second definition can
be extended in a natural way to give a general notion of surface relations
which would not depend on inflectional richness of languages as the first
one does. This second general notion of surface relation would, more-
over, impose a natural limit on the number of definable ones, since there
would be at most as many surface relations as underlying relations,

with all of the surface relations defined from the base relations in terms of substitution transformations exactly as the surface subject was defined from the base subject.

2.3 Underlying Subject and Transitive-Intransitive Verb Pairs

2.30 Subjectless sentences

Some interesting problems arise if we look a little more closely at some of the things which were tacitly assumed above to be underlying subjects.[17] Consider first the following sentences:

(2-28)   John has broken the window.

(2-29)   The window has broken.

(2-30)   The window has been broken.

(Sentence (2-30) is to be considered only as a passive; the interpretation of "broken" as an adjective, if possible at all with this choice of auxiliary, does not relate to the present discussion.) The third sentence is a passive with deleted agent phrase, which can be assumed to be transformationally derived from "X has broken the window", where X may be variously argued to be (i) the word "someone", (ii) an abstract bundle of features containing whatever is common to all subjects of the verb "break", or (iii) a completely unspecified NP. All of these correspond essentially to the remark that the third sentence has a deleted indefinite underlying subject.

---

17. Many of the points in the ensuing discussion were first brought to my attention by T.M. Lightner. I am also grateful to have had a chance to present some of these ideas for discussion at a graduate linguistics group meeting at UCLA, and for fruitful discussions with Professors N. Chomsky, E. Klima, and P. Postal, and with J.R. Ross, P.S. Rosenbaum, R.P.V. Kiparsky, J. Gruber, and others. This does not necessarily imply that any of them agree with me.

The second sentence is not semantically identical to the third, and

hence must not have an identical underlying structure. Whereas the third

sentence definitely conveys the idea that the window was broken by some

active agent but gives no information about what that agent was, the

second sentence is even more indefinite in that it does not indicate

whether any outside agent was involved or not. The following excerpts

support this distinction:

> "But these two passive forms are often not identical in force.
> The passive with passive form represents a person or thing
> as being affected by an agent working under resistance vigor-
> ously and consciously to a definite end [this is perhaps a
> little strong - BH] , while the passive with intransitive form
> represents an activity as proceeding easily, naturally, often
> almost spontaneously."[18]

> "The chairman began the meeting promptly.
> The meeting began promptly.
> The meeting was begun promptly.

> In the second sentence there is no hint of an awareness of
> an active agent, apart from the meeting itself, responsible
> for the meeting's beginning. In the third sentence there is
> such an awareness."[19]

The question is then what the difference is in the underlying struc-

ture of the sentences which determines their differences in semantic

interpretation. If one were to say that "break" is transitive in (2-28)

and (2-30) but intransitive in (2-29), then one would be missing the

important generalization that whatever can be an object in the transi-

tive case can be subject in the intransitive case[20], the same generali-

---

18. Curme, Syntax, p. 441.

19. Ralph B. Long, The Sentence and Its Parts (Chicago: The Univ. of
     Chicago Press, 1961) p. 116.

20. There are a few marginal exceptions such as "break a record", but
     the generalization holds in the vast majority of cases. The class
     of verbs which behave this way is very large, including, for
     instance, "bend", "move", "burn", "stop", "turn".

zation which is used in arguing for deriving passive sentences transformationally from active ones. A more plausible suggestion might be
that "break" is in all cases an intransitive verb, and sentences (2-28)
and (2-30) are "causatives" rather than simple transitives. The first
sentence might be postulated to have roughly the following underlying
structure:

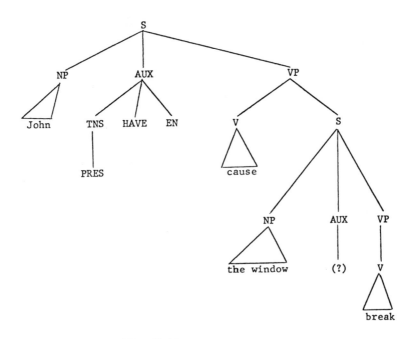

Fig. 2-ii

Then probably a causative transformation which is independent of the
verb in the complement sentence would give "John has caused the window
to break", and a subsequent transformation which applies only to verbs

of this class would optionally transform that into "John has broken the window". The first of these two transformations is clearly necessary regardless of the analysis we give to sentences with verbs like "break" in them; it is probably the same transformation that operates with verbs like "expect". However, there are a number of arguments against using this construction as a basis for deriving transitive "break". One argument which probably does not convince anyone who does not already agree is that causing a window to break and breaking a window simply do not mean the same thing. This can be backed up, however, with the stronger argument that there are actual differences in the expressions which can occur as subjects of "-- cause NP to V" and "-- V NP":

(2-31)   A change in molecular structure caused the window to break.

(2-32)   *A change in molecular structure broke the window.

(2-33)   The low air pressure caused the water to boil.

(2-34)   *The low air pressure boiled the water.

(2-35)   The angle at which the door was mounted caused it to open whenever it wasn't latched.

(2-36)   *The angle at which the door was mounted opened it whenever it wasn't latched.

The non-sentences (2-32), (2-34), (2-36) could be avoided by requiring the subject of "cause" to be animate when embedding is to take place. An alternative suggestion is that it is not actually the specific verb "cause" that is involved, but rather a dummy verb with the essential causative features. The dummy verb would obligatorily undergo the embedding transformation.

Another possibility is that "break" and the other verbs of that class are basically transitive, i.e. always require a following NP in the underlying structure, but that they do not require a subject. This entails changing the first rule of the grammar from (ignoring PRE for the time being)

$$S \longrightarrow NP \quad AUX \quad VP$$

to

$$S \longrightarrow (NP) \quad AUX \quad VP.$$

Just as the complex symbol for verbs has always been assumed to contain information as to whether a given verb requires a following NP or not, it will now have to contain information as to whether it requires a preceding NP.[21] The underlying form of sentence (2-29) would then be as follows:

---

21. It may turn out that the preceding NP is optional only for transitive verbs, in which case only transitive verbs would be specified for this feature, and a redundancy rule would specify the preceding NP as obligatory for other verbs. In either case, the marking of verbs for whether or not they require a subject NP violates a generalization about subcategorization features which has been suggested by Chomsky, namely that constituents can be subcategorized only with respect to other constituents immediately dominated by the same node that dominates the given constituent. (Aspects of the Theory of Syntax.)

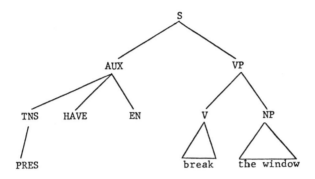

Fig. 2-iii

Note especially that "break" and "the window" stand in the same relation in this structure as in the underlying structure for (2-28) or (2-30). A simple transformation applies very early and preposes the object if there is no subject:

TSUBJ (i)   (obligatory):

$$\#\# - AUX - V - NP \implies 1 - 4 - 2 - 3$$

This transformation is somewhat simpler than the one which would be required in the analysis based on causatives. This analysis furthermore provides a natural basis for the feeling that in (2-30) there is an agent involved which is simply left unspecified but that in (2-29) there is not necessarily an agent involved at all. Note incidentally that even without going into any detail about the form of lexical entries, one can see that the entry for a verb like "break" is no more complicated under this analysis than it would be under the causative analysis; in the latter, each intransitive verb would need a feature

specifying whether or not it could undergo the transitivizing transformation; in the analysis defended here, there is instead the equivalent of a feature in that each transitive verb is now marked for whether
or not it requires a subject.

The usefulness of the proposed rules does not end with the passive-
intransitive distinction, however. Consider next the following sentences:

(2-37)   John broke the window with the hammer.

(2-38)   The hammer broke the window.

(2-39)   *The hammer broke the window with John.

Note also that if one accepts

(2-40)   James Bond broke the window with the Russian (by hurling
          him through it).

then one will also regard the following as ambiguous:

(2-41)   The Russian broke the window.

Any NP in an instrumental with-phrase can be used as a subject with
the same class of verbs discussed above, while not every subject can be
used in a with-phrase. This fact can be accounted for with a few simple
modifications in the rules proposed above. In the phrase structure
rules the with-phrase will be introduced preceding the object:[22]

$$VP \longrightarrow V \quad (\text{with NP}) \quad (NP).$$

---

22. The object is optional, since there are intransitive verbs which
     can have instrumental with-phrases: "He walks with a cane,"
     "He thinks with his heart instead of with his head," and
     "He floated with an inner tube."

Then the underlying forms of (2-37) and (2-38) will be, respectively:

(2-42)   ## John - broke - with the hammer - the window ##

(2-43)   ##   broke - with the hammer - the window ##

The first of these can be restored to correct word order by a simple

transformation:

TOBJORD (obligatory):

$$V - Prep\ NP - NP \implies 1 - 3 - 2$$
$$1 \quad\ \ 2 \qquad 3$$

The second sentence requires that TSUBJ be modified slightly:

TSUBJ (ii) (obligatory):

$$\#\# - AUX - V - (Prep) - NP \implies 1\text{-}5\text{+}2\text{-}3\text{-}\emptyset\text{-}\emptyset$$
$$1 \quad\ \ 2 \quad\ 3 \qquad 4 \qquad 5$$

The analysis just proposed fails to account for the restrictions on

the occurrence of certain types of adverbial phrases, as in the sentences

below:

(2-44)   John broke the window deliberately.

(2-45)   *The window broke deliberately.

(2-46)   The glass broke from being stepped on.

(2-47)   *John broke the glass from being stepped on.

It would increase the complexity of the analysis prohibitively to

try to have the form of such adverbials be determined by the presence

or absence of an underlying subject. On the other hand, the causative

analysis is not entirely satisfactory in this respect either, since

these sentences could be accommodated only by making the causative embedding dependent on the absence of certain adverbial phrases from the embedded sentence. The adverbs in question seem to depend on both the verb and whatever constituent ends up as surface subject; since it is not clear what sort of analysis can account for this phenomenon, the analysis with subjectless sentences will be tentatively maintained so that its further consequences can be explored, but it is clear that it must either be improved greatly or eventually abandoned.

2.31 "The car drives easily."

Verbs like "drive", which can be used intransitively only with a manner adverbial, do require a subject which can, however, be deleted when it is indefinite if there is a manner adverbial. Sentences such as

(2-48)   The car drives easily.

differ semantically from (2-29) in that the involvement of an outside agent is definitely implied.

Verbs such as "hit" and "strike" are like "break" in that a with-phrase can become the subject, but differ from "break" in that the direct object cannot become the subject.

(2-49)   John struck the window with the hammer.

(2-50)   The hammer struck the window.

(2-51)   *The window struck.

If the analysis with subjectless sentences is used, it will be necessary to specify a verb such as "strike" as requiring either an underlying subject or a with-phrase, and permitting both. The necessity for such a specification is a serious problem for the proposed analysis and one for which no solution is apparent.

2.32 Causatives.

In sentences such as the following, the intransitive member of each pair seems intuitively to be more basic than the transitive one, in contrast with the sentences with "break", etc.:

(2-53)   The dog was walking.

(2-54)   I was walking the dog.

(2-55)   The horse galloped.

(2-56)   I galloped the horse.

(2-57)   The corn grew.

(2-58)   The farmer grew the corn.

The class of verbs of this sort (they are distinguished from the "break" class by the fact that these can all take animate subjects in the in- transitive use -- e.g. "John grew" is possible as well as "the corn grew") is substantially smaller than the "break" class, and it might even be argued that they are not a real class at all but a superficially similar collection of idiosyncratic items. For instance, semantically

I walked the dog. = I took the dog for a walk. ≠ I made the dog walk.

I galloped the horse. = I made the horse gallop. ≠ I took the horse for a gallop.

The farmer grew the corn. ≠ The farmer made the corn grow. ≠ *The farmer took the corn for a grow.

I walked John to the corner. ≠ I took John for a walk to the corner. ≠ I made John walk to the corner.

*The farmer grew John.

The number of verbs that refer to horses' gaits is probably large enough to warrant setting up some sort of a transformation relating the transitive and intransitive uses, since they all work like "gallop". One could, of course assign these verbs to the "break" class (except for "grow"), and in fact unless some syntactic reasons can be found for giving them a different analysis, considerations of simplicity will require that analysis. It will then be left to the semantic component to account for the intuitively felt difference between the two classes. It seems more reasonable to hope that a purely syntactic argument will be found for making the intransitive forms the underlying ones in these cases, however.

2.33 Animacy of underlying subjects.

It may be noticed that using the rules so far introduced, almost all underlying subjects of transitive verbs are animate (since in sentences like "The hammer broke the window", "the hammer" is no longer considered the underlying subject.) One of the largest classes of apparent exceptions is the class of "affective verbs" such as "surprise" and "frighten", which require animate objects, but which can take almost anything, including nominalizations, as subject. These verbs are already known to have a number of special properties, e.g., they normally cannot be used in the progressive, but do form true adjectives in -ing:

(2-59)   *Dark rooms are frightening me.

(2-60)   Dark rooms are very frightening.

However, note that with an animate subject, such verbs can be used in
the progressive:

(2-61) John is frightening the baby.

Furthermore, when used with a neutral auxiliary and an animate subject,
such verbs lead to an ambiguity.

(2-62) John frightened the baby.

cf.

(2-63) John frightened the baby because she wasn't used to him.

(2-64) John frightened the baby because he liked to see her cry.

Let us refer to these two interpretations as "active" (2-61, 2-64) and
stative (2-63). There are at least three possible ways of making two
different underlying structures for the two different readings of (2-62):
by a difference in the subjects, a difference in the verbs, or a difference in the objects (or any combination of these), and unfortunately
there are conflicting arguments in favor of different solutions.

(i) The subject in the stative case might come from an underlying
instrumental with-phrase in a sentence of the active type, parallel to
"the hammer broke the window". This is supported by the following pairs
of sentences, which are certainly related:

(2-65) John annoyed Mary with his persistence.

(2-66) John's persistence annoyed Mary.

(2-67) Bill frightened Tom with the gun.

(2-68) The gun frightened Tom.

(2-69)   Paul convinced Peter of the truth of the theorem with
         his elegant proof.

(2-70)   Paul's elegant proof convinced Peter of the truth of
         the theorem.

There is a similar relation with by-phrases; it is not clear whether
these are the same as with-phrases or not.

(2-71)   John surprised Mary by remembering her birthday.

(2-72)   John's remembering Mary's birthday surprised her.

(ii)   The verbs have several different properties in the two uses,
which might be rather difficult to state if one use is derived from the
other.   One difference, the possible use with progressive in the active
case but not in the stative, has already been mentioned.   Another difference appears in nominalizations.

(2-73)   Bill's annoying Mary was a scandal.

(2-74)   *The gift's annoying Mary ...

(2-75)   Its annoying Mary ...

(2-76)   Mary's annoyance at the gift ...

(2-77)   *The gift's annoyance of Mary ...

(2-78)   *Bill's annoyance of Mary ...

That is, the active sentences can take a normal Possessive - Ing nominalization, but some stative ones cannot ((2-75) but not (2-76)).   The
stative forms of many of these verbs occur in a construction in which the
possessive morpheme is attached to the __object__, Lees's nominalizing
morpheme Nml[23] is attached to the verb, and the subject follows, preceded

---

23.   Robert B. Lees, The Grammar of English Nominalizations [hereafter GEN]
      (Bloomington: Publication Twelve of the Indiana University Research
      Center in Anthropology, Folklore, and Linguistics, 1960), p. 68.

by some preposition, usually "at" and never "by". (This differs from Lees's genitive periphrasis of Action Nominals[24] both in not having an underlying simple Action Nominal, *the gift's annoyance of Mary, and in not having "by" as the preposition before the subject.) Some other examples of stative nominalizations are:

(2-79)   Mary's fear of the dark

(2-80)   Mary's surprise at John's arrival

(2-81)   Mary's alarm at the news

(2-82)   Mary's amusement at our predicament

(cf. (2-83)   John's appointment by the committee)

(iii)   The passives suggest that there may be a difference in the underlying structure of the objects in the two cases:

(2-84)   Mary was frightened (with a gun) by John.

(2-85)   *Mary was frightened by the dark woods. (acceptable for some speakers)

(2-86)   Mary was frightened of the dark woods.

If "Mary" were simply a direct object in the stative case, we should expect to get the starred sentence (2-85). Also note that although we don't have

(2-87)   *The dark forest was frightening Mary.

we do have

(2-88)   The dark forest was frightening to Mary.

---

24. GEN, pp. 67-68.

But this is not simply a to + NP following the verb as in

    (2-89)   John was talking to Mary.

because there is no

    (2-90)   *The dark forest frightened to Mary.

It is not at all clear how verbs like "frighten" are to be analyzed. On the surface they certainly appear to be counterexamples to the claim that all underlying subjects of transitive verbs are animate, but the problems raised here suggest that deeper analysis is required before it will be possible to use these verbs as conclusive refutation of the claim.

2.34 Exceptions to § 2.33

There are some other verbs which appear to be exceptions to the claim that all subjects of transitive verbs are animate; they will not be analyzed in detail here, but they also seem to be rather special in various ways, and it does not seem improbable that deeper analysis will show them to have some other underlying structure than simple subject - verb - object.[25]

subtend	cause	emit
exceed	preclude	exude
precede	occasion	reflect
transcend	entail	refract
approach	indicate	
	mean	

---

25. Most of these examples are due to J.R. Ross.

2.4 Consequences of Subjectless Sentences.

Since the two transformations TSUBJ and TOBJORD operate as very
early rules, the statement of most of the other rules is just as it
would have been if all of the structures concerned had been derived
directly in the phrase structure component (missing the important
generalizations noted above, of course.) There are considerable reper-
cussions of these changes on the notions of underlying and surface subjects, however. It might first of all be suggested that the traditional
notion "agent" corresponds very closely to "underlying subject of a
transitive verb" in the grammar containing the rules of §2.3. What was
called underlying subject in §2.0 was the relation (NP, S), which corresponds fairly closely to what was often called "logical subject" in the
past. Although the underlying subject can still be defined as (NP, S),
the extension of the relation has changed significantly (for instance,
some sentences now have no underlying subject at all) and no longer
accords with any particular traditional notion.

If this syntactic analysis is correct, one must conclude that the
traditional notion of logical subject did not represent any significant
aspect of the structure that speakers of English impose on their
language.

CHAPTER III

VERB AND OBJECT

3.0 The Determination of Underlying Structure

In this chapter, the basic distinctions will be drawn between under-

lying and derived objects and among the main types of objects. The

first section contains a discussion of some of the factors which are

relevant to determining underlying structure within the verb phrase.

3.01 Reflexivization

A number of people have pointed out (see for instance Lees,

GEN, 99-102) that reflexivization occurs when two identical noun phrases

are in the same constituent sentence, and not when one is in a sentence

embedded in the sentence containing the other. This generalization can

be seen most clearly from examples such as the following:

(3-1)   John forced me to shoot myself.

(3-2)   *John forced me to shoot me.

(3-3)   *John forced me to shoot himself.

(3-4)   I forced myself to shoot John.

(3-5)   *I forced me to shoot John.

In these examples, the underlying structure is roughly as follows:

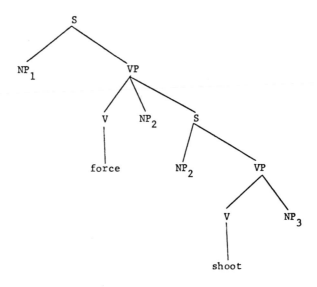

Fig. 3-i

If $NP_1 = NP_2$, NP_2 is reflexivized; if $NP_2 = NP_3$, NP_3 is reflexivized; but if $NP_1 = NP_3$, reflexivization does not take place, because the two noun phrases are not in the same minimal S, where the term minimal S refers to an S and the structure below it exclusive of the structure below any lower S's.

If true, this observation would provide a fruitful test in many cases for determining whether some apparent object of a verb is a constituent of that verb phrase in the underlying structure or is transformationally introduced from some embedded sentence. For instance, from a consideration of the pronouns in the following sentences:

(3-6)   I kept the gun near me.

(3-7)   I kept myself near the door.

(3-8)   I aimed the gun at myself.

(3-9)   I aimed myself at the quarterback.

one would conclude that in sentences (3-6) and (3-7), the first NP after

the verb is an underlying constituent of the minimal S containing the

subject but the second NP comes rather from an embedded structure some-

thing like:

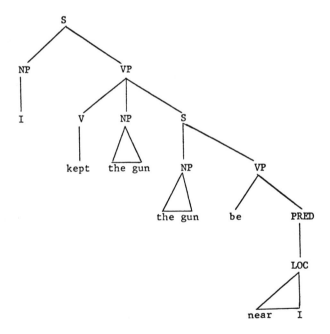

Fig. 3-11

In sentences (3-8) and (3-9), on the other hand, one would conclude that both the noun phrase immediately following the verb and the at-phrase are underlying constituents of a single minimal S.

3.011

There are, however, some apparent exceptions to the rule that reflexivization occurs only within minimal S's. Only if reflexivization can be accounted for in all cases where there are independent grounds for establishing a certain constituent structure is one justified in using reflexivization as a key to structure in other cases, such as the sentences above. The following sentences illustrate some of the problems that must be settled.[1]

(3-10)   The only thing John talks to Mary about is <u>himself</u>.

(3-11)   The only thing John talks to Mary about is <u>herself</u>.

(3-12)   John's favorite topic of conversation is <u>himself</u>.

(3-13)   Many of John's pictures are of <u>himself</u>.

In sentences (3-10) and (3-11), both "John" and "Mary" are in a relative clause modifying "thing", while the reflexivized element is in the predicate of the kernel containing "thing". In (3-12), "John" is in a genitive phrase modifying the subject while the reflexive is in a predicate NP; (3-13) is similar, except that the reflexivized element is not so clearly in the predicate of the same minimal S, since of-phrases have very restricted occurrence in predicate position. In all

---

1.   Seeming counterexamples of the opposite sort, in which reflexivization does not take place although it would seem that it should, such as "He drew Mary toward him", are discussed below in §3.32.

these cases, then, the analysis one would arrive at on the basis of the
reflexivization rule disagrees with the analysis one would posit on
other syntactic grounds; so either the latter analyses or the reflexivization rule must not be quite right. But are these really the only
alternatives? No; there may be another source for -self pronouns
besides the reflexivization rule. This possibility will be examined
first.

3.0111

One characteristic of these problematical uses of the -self
pronoun is that they have main stress. In this respect they are like
the appositive -self pronouns:

(3-14)   John will wash the car himself.

(3-15)   They took their petition to the President himself.

(3-16)   I would stay away from them, myself.

(3-17)   Oh, you've been to Tokyo? I've been there myself.

A little closer examination of the appositive -self pronouns may help to
clarify the apparent reflexives in sentences (3-10) - (3-13). The four
sentences above illustrate four different uses of the -self pronoun,
although all are appositive. The semantic differences can be roughly
indicated by the approximate paraphrases:

(3-18)   John will wash the car alone, without assistance.

(3-19)   They took their petition to the President, no less.

(3-20)   I would stay away from them if I were you.

(3-21)   Oh, you've been to Tokyo? I've been there, too.

There are also syntactic differences; it has been stated that any appositive -self pronoun can appear either just after the noun it repeats or at the end of the sentence.[2] It seems at first blush, for instance, that (3-14) is a free variant of

(3-22)   John himself will wash the car.

But it is not the case that any -self pronoun that can appear in one position can appear in the other; "oneself" can appear only at the end of a sentence, and when a passive sentence has a -self pronoun immediately following the subject, that pronoun cannot be moved to the end of the sentence.

(3-23)   With proper tools, one can assemble a bicycle oneself.

(3-24)   *With proper tools, one oneself can assemble a bicycle.

(3-25)   The President himself was implicated in the scandal.

(3-26)   *The President was implicated in the scandal himself.

These two pairs of sentences show that (3-14) and (3-15) represent uses of the -self pronoun which are syntactically as well as semantically distinct. Sentence (3-16) is syntactically distinct from both of these in that the first person singular is the only possibility for such a construction.

(3-27)   I would make John do it himself, myself.

(3-28)   *She would make John do it himself, herself.

Furthermore, there are sentences which are identical except for intonation (reflected in the difference in punctuation):

2.   Jespersen, MEG VII, 171: "The former position is somewhat more pretentious and perhaps more literary, the latter, in which the pronoun comes as a kind of afterthought, is frequent in colloquial speech."

(3-29)   I wouldn't tell John about that myself; I'd get someone
         more tactful to do it.

(3-30)   I wouldn't tell John about that, myself; he might worry
         if he knew.

Sentence (3-17) exemplifies a use which is like that in (3-15) in that

the passive is possible, but unlike it in that the -self pronoun can be

only at the end of the sentence, not next to the noun.

(3-31)   I know the store you mean; I've been gypped there a few
         times myself.

(3-32)   I know the store you mean; I myself have been gypped
         there a few times.

These two sentences, although both grammatical, are not synonymous; the

first has the "me, too" meaning of (3-17), and the second the "even I"

meaning of (3-15).

3.0112

Although these four uses of the -self pronouns are all distinct,

they have in common an element of emphasis. They are all roughly equiva-

lent to sentences in which the -self pronoun is omitted and the noun or

pronoun which it repeated is given heavy stress, although such a rough

equivalent may turn out to be ambiguous (as in (3-29) and (3-30), and in

(3-31) and (3-32)). Now notice that sentences (3-10) - (3-13) are

paraphrases of, respectively:

(3-33)   The only thing John talks to Mary about is John himself.

(3-34)   The only thing John talks to Mary about is Mary herself.

(3-35)   John's favorite topic of conversation is John himself.

(3-36)   Many of John's pictures are of John himself.

Sentences (3-33) - (3-36) sound rather awkward, and perhaps for some speakers the rules given below which convert them to (3-10) - (3-13) are obligatory. But in sentences where the pronoun alone would be ambiguous, the repeated noun sounds quite natural:

(3-37)   The only thing John talks to Bill about is $\begin{Bmatrix} John \\ Bill \end{Bmatrix}$ himself.

Ordinary minimal S reflexives, on the other hand, cannot be so paraphrased under any circumstances:

(3-38)   *John persuaded Bill to shoot Bill himself.

It might be postulated, then, that sentences (3-10) - (3-13) are really cases of the appositive -self pronoun, and not simple reflexives like those in sentences (3-1) - (3-5). Without an attempt at an exact specification of the rules for introducing appositive -self pronouns, it is proposed that sentences (3-33) - (3-36) represent an earlier stage in the derivation of (3-10) - (3-13), a stage reached before the pronominalization rule applies. Ordinary pronominalization takes place regardless of the level of embedding of the parts of a sentence:

(3-39)   John assured Mary that he would return the book that he had borrowed from her.

Hence pronominalization would yield from sentence (3-33):

(3-40)   The only thing John talks to Mary about is him himself.

Corresponding forms would be obtained from (3-34) - (3-36). Then the only other rule needed to account for (3-10) - (3-13) is an obligatory rule to delete the non-self pronoun before the corresponding -self pronoun:

<u>TPRODEL</u> (obligatory):

$$X - PRO + N - PRO + N + SELF - Y \implies 1\text{-}\emptyset\text{-}\emptyset\text{-}4\text{+}5\text{+}6\text{-}7$$
$$1 \quad 2 \quad 3 \quad 4 \quad 5 \quad 6 \quad 7$$

Condition: 3 = 5

The discussion has purposely been kept independent of the exact formulation of pronominalization, which is not under consideration here.
There is one specific feature of pronominalization, however, which
deserves mention at this point. It has been suggested[3] that pronouns
used as independent nouns have a structure distinct from that of pronouns
formed by the pronominalization transformation from repeated nouns. New
evidence in support of this claim is provided by the fact that TPRODEL
does not apply to independent pronouns, as in:

(3-41)   He himself has told a lie on occasion.

3.012

If this account of the apparent reflexives in sentences
(3-10) - (3-13) is correct, then one is justified in continuing to consider reflexivization a valid indicator of whether two constituents are
in the same minimal S or not. However, because the conditions under
which appositive -self pronouns can appear have not been determined, and
because there is not really a black-and-white distinction in the gram-
maticality of sentences (3-33) - (3-36) as opposed to (3-38), a clear
test for telling whether a given -self pronoun is a reflexive or an
appositive has not actually been established.

Furthermore, there are certain facts which shed doubt on the validity
of even this incomplete and tentative account of the -self pronouns in

3.   Lees, <u>GEN</u>, p. 100.

sentences (3-10) - (3-13). One of these is the contrast in the following pairs of sentences:

(3-42)   I dislike that picture of myself.

(3-43)   I dislike Mary's picture of me.

(3-44)   I dislike adverse comments about myself.

(3-45)   I dislike Mary's comments about me.

There is nothing in the analysis offered above that would account for the difference in reflexivization in these sentences. While it is true that the following are also possible:

(3-46)   I dislike that picture of me.

(3-47)   I dislike adverse comments about me.

there is still a problem, because some explanation is needed for why the following are not possible as variants of (3-42) and (3-44):

(3-48)   *I dislike Mary's picture of myself.

(3-49)   *I dislike Mary's comments about myself.

It will nevertheless be assumed that there is a reflexivization rule which depends on minimal S structure and its consequences will be used, to the extent that they can be discovered, as support, although not as conclusive evidence, for analyzing various constituents as being in the same or different minimal S's.

One of the reasons for going into such detail in what turns out to be a rather inconclusive argument is to try to make it at least plausible that the apparent exceptions to the generalization about the reflexive rule are not due to any defect in that rule itself but to another source for -self pronouns; the examples given are those which appear most likely to be fruitful for obtaining deeper insights into the other uses of the -self pronouns.

3.02 Co-occurrence relations

The main consideration in determining whether a certain constituent is introduced in the phrase structure or by transformation is, of course, relations among different sentences. If some pair of constituents in one kind of sentence have exactly or very nearly the same co-occurrence restrictions as some other pair in a sentence of another kind, then it is very likely that at least one of those constituents is introduced transformationally into at least one of those sentence types, since otherwise those co-occurrence restrictions would have to be stated twice in the phrase structure component of the grammar.

It is not necessary to go into any detail on this point; it is discussed widely in the literature on transformational grammar[4]. It is mentioned here simply to prevent the impression that one should rely primarily on such special indicators as reflexivization in determining underlying structure. In general it is not possible to find any necessary and sufficient condition for whether two constituents are in the same minimal S; the best one can do is compare the overall results in terms of the whole grammar of incorporating one or another of the possible decisions in any particular case.

---

4.   See, e.g., Zellig S. Harris, "Co-occurrence and Transformation in Linguistic Structure," Language, 33, No.3 (July-September 1957), 283-340. Reprinted in Jerry A. Fodor & Jerrold J. Katz, eds., The Structure of Language: Readings in the Philosophy of Language (Englewood Cliffs: Prentice-Hall, Inc., 1964), 155-210.

3.1 Direct Object

The fact that verbs are traditionally divided into two major classes, transitive and intransitive, shows that the notion of direct object has generally been considered fundamental in the description of the structure of the verb phrase. It is clear that direct objects are part of the underlying structure, since (a) given a verb which occurs in a simple sentence consisting of subject, verb, and direct object, there is generally no other simpler or equally simple sentence form which has the same co-occurrence restrictions between the noun phrases which can occur in the direct object position and the verb, and (b) direct objects always reflexivize.

However, the preceding statement presupposes that direct objects are well-defined and recognizable constituents. Such a presupposition is based on a number of characteristics shared by the most universally accepted cases of direct objects, but since there are constructions which have some of these characteristics but lack others, there naturally arises the question of which properties are fundamental to the notion of direct object or even whether in fact the notion is as well-defined as it has generally been assumed to be.

The terms "object", "complement", and "predicate nominative" are all derived from classical grammars and do not necessarily provide the best description of English sentence structure. In English a more natural description might be in terms of noun phrases governed directly by the verb as opposed to those governed obliquely, or indirectly. A noun phrase in a with-phrase, for instance, may be considered obliquely governed by the verb if the with-phrase is itself governed directly by the verb. Most noun phrases which have traditionally been called "complements" of the verb are contained in some phrase governed directly by the verb which can have other elements such as a preposition in it as well as the noun phrase, and thus such noun phrases are governed obliquely by the verb. The traditional predicate nominative is a noun phrase which, although it forms a phrase by itself without any accompanying constituents, can be seen to belong to a larger phrase-type "Predicate", since there are a number of other constituents which can occur instead of the noun phrase after "be"; i.e., the construction is not "be NP", but "be PRED", where PRED dominates NP. Thus predicate nominatives can be considered to be governed obliquely by "be".

If it turns out that there is only one NP which is ever immediately dominated by the same constituent which dominates the verb (assume for the time being that that constituent is VP^5), then the direct object relation can be defined as (NP, VP); i.e., as the only noun phrase governed directly rather than obliquely by the verb. If it should turn

---

5. The question of how the verb phrase is broken down into constituents on different levels, such as MV, Vb, V, etc., is ignored in this section, since the main factors which determine such a hierarchy are the behavior of various parts of the verb phrase under transformations such as passive, questions, and nominalizations, not treated here. Any rule in this chapter of the form

    VP -----→   A B C

could be replaced by a pair of rules such as

    VP -----→   MV C

    MV -----→   A B

without affecting the arguments or conclusions given in this section.

out that more than one NP can be dominated directly by VP, then some more complex means of representing relations will have to be devised if a direct object relation is to be maintained.

The problems concerning direct objects whose consideration is being neglected include apparently simple objects of verbs which cannot be passivized such as "resemble" and "suit", cognate objects such as "die a noble death", and deletable objects.

3.2 Indirect Objects

Indirect objects have been characterized traditionally by their permutability with direct objects and the appearance of "to" or "for" when they follow the direct object. Although at first glance they would appear to be just as much a part of the underlying structure of the verb phrase as direct objects, there are actually fairly strong arguments against that view, as well as some serious arguments in its favor.

3.21 Underlying structure of indirect objects

In support of considering indirect objects to be transforma-tionally derived is the fact that for many verbs which take an indirect and a direct object there exists a verb whose subject and object respec-tively have essentially identical co-occurrence restrictions. For in-stance, for every sentence of the form

(3-50)   NP told NP' NP" (or NP told NP" to NP')

there exists a sentence

(3-51)   NP' heard NP"

(although there is not always a sentence of the form of (3-50) for each one of the form (3-51).)

Other such pairs of verbs include:

give	-	have
show	-	see
sell	-	buy
feed	-	eat
send	-	receive
throw	-	catch

In all these cases, there is a strong semantic connection between the members of the verb pairs which adds plausibility to the suggestion that such pairs of sentences be considered transformationally related. Such a sentence as

(3-52)   The farmer fed the horses oats.

might be derived from an underlying form something like:

(3-53)   The farmer- $\begin{bmatrix} V \\ \text{causative} \end{bmatrix}$ - $\begin{bmatrix} \text{the horses ate oats} \end{bmatrix}_S$

where the main verb is an unspecified causative.

3.22

If all the verbs which take indirect objects could be uniquely paired with appropriate single-object verbs, there would still be two problems raised by attempting such derivations.

One of the problems is that indirect objects do reflexivize, and accordingly their transformational derivation would be the only counter-example to the claim, supported above, that reflexivization occurs only in minimal S's. The other problem concerns the form of the transformations that would be required for such derivations and the status of the derived verbs. Either there would have to be as many transformations as

there are verb pairs with each transformation introducing the appropriate
verb, or there would be a single transformation which adds the features
of the single-object verb into the $\begin{bmatrix} V \\ \text{causative} \end{bmatrix}$ matrix, and then there
would have to be a morphophonemic rule which rewrote "eat" as "feed",
"hear" as "tell", etc., in the environment of the feature "causative".
In either case the verbs "give", "feed", "show", etc., would not appear
in the lexicon, or at most they would appear as alternants of "have",
"eat", "see", etc. Postulating a derivational relation in cases like
these seems much less natural than the more usual cases such as having
"redden" derive from "red", where the morphological relation is clear,
or considering "went" an alternant of "go" on the grounds that this
pair is an exceptional member of a pattern which shows clear morphological relations in its regular members.

3.23

Although such problems may have to be faced in other contexts,
it is not necessary to try to resolve them here, because there is the
much more fundamental objection that there are numerous examples of verbs
taking indirect objects for which there is no apparent corresponding
simple direct-object verb. A glance at the list of indirect-object verbs
in Jespersen MEG,III, Chapter 14, for instance, reveals that in the vast
majority of cases there is not a unique corresponding single-object verb;
either no appropriate verb exists, or there are several possibilities,
the choice among which would have to be arbitrary.

3.24

The considerations above provide evidence against considering indirect object constructions transformationally derived from sentences with a direct object but shed no particular light on what the underlying structure of indirect objects actually is.

3.241

Since nearly all indirect objects can occur either before the direct object without a preposition or after the direct object preceded by "to" or "for", it would seem most natural to take one of these positions as the position of indirect objects in the underlying structure. The two forms could be transformationally related most simply if the "to" or "for" were introduced in the underlying structure and deleted by a transformation, since there is no simple means for predicting which preposition occurs. Some verbs, in fact, can be used with either:

(3-54)   John wrote us a new play.

(3-55)   John wrote a new play for us.

(3-56)   *John wrote a new play to us.

(3-57)   John wrote Mary a postcard.

(3-58)   John wrote a postcard to Mary.

(3-59)   John wrote a postcard for Mary.

Sentence (3-59), although a perfectly good sentence, can be shown to be unrelated to sentence (3-57) for syntactic as well as the obvious semantic reasons; the "for Mary" of sentence (3-59) can co-occur with an indirect object, while the "to Mary" of (3-58) cannot.

- 58 -

(3-60)   *John wrote Bill a postcard to Mary.

(3-61)   John wrote Bill a postcard for Mary.

With sentences (3-55) and (3-58) regarded as underlying (3-54) and
(3-57) respectively as well as themselves, the indirect object transformation would be as follows:

TIO (optional)

$$X - V - NP - \left\{ \begin{matrix} to \\ for \end{matrix} \right\} - NP - Y \implies 1\text{-}2\text{-}5\text{+}3\text{-}\emptyset\text{-}\emptyset\text{-}6$$
$$1 \quad 2 \quad 3 \qquad 4 \qquad 5 \quad 6$$

Condition: 5 dominates $\begin{bmatrix} N \\ +animate \end{bmatrix}^6$

3.242

It would also be possible to have in the underlying representation the noun phrase with the preposition but in the position of the
prepositionless form, before the direct object. Considered in isolation,
such a description would appear to be more complicated than that suggested in §3.241, since two transformations would be required, one to
place the Prep + NP phrase after the direct object and the other to
delete the preposition if the Prep + NP phrase precedes the direct object.
The two rules can be put in either order as long as whichever comes first
is optional and whichever comes second is obligatory. However, if the
preposition deletion rule is placed first (and hence made optional),
then the other rule need not be stated separately at all, since it is
already included in TOBJORD, given in §2.3. TOBJORD was needed because

---

6.   The exceptions to this condition, such as "I gave the house a coat
     of paint", are discussed below in §3.25.

with-phrases must precede direct objects in the underlying structure to allow the simplest formulation of TSUBJ, and the with-phrase must then be moved to the right of the direct object if the sentence has an underlying subject. Essentially the same formulation of TOBJORD can move the indirect object to the right of the direct object if the preposition is not deleted.[7] Since the preposition deletion rule is simpler than the indirect object rule TIO required by the analysis of §3.241, the analysis with the preposition deletion rule is to be preferred. This analysis entails the following phrase structure and transformational rules:

$$VP \longrightarrow V \ \ (with \ NP) \ \ (\ (\left\{ {to \atop for} \right\} \ NP \ ) \ NP)$$

TIOPREPDEL (optional; precedes TOBJORD)

$$X - V - Y - \left\{ {to \atop for} \right\} - NP - NP - Z \implies 1\text{-}2\text{-}3\text{-}\emptyset\text{-}5\text{-}6\text{-}7$$
$$1 \quad 2 \quad 3 \qquad 4 \qquad \quad 5 \quad \ 6 \quad 7$$

Condition: 5 dominates $\begin{bmatrix} N \\ +animate \end{bmatrix}$

The string (3-62) therefore underlies both (3-54) and (3-55), and (3-63) underlies both (3-57) and (3-58).

(3-62)   John wrote for us a new play.

(3-63)   John wrote to Mary a postcard.

3.25

However, if (3-62) and (3-63) are regarded as underlying (3-54) and (3-57), a problem arises from the fact that not all instances of

---

7.   Certain modifications are required in TOBJORD to account for "I wrote a letter to John with a new pen" and other constructions which are discussed below. In §3.33 these are summarized and the revised rule is given.

"to NP" and "for NP" following a direct object alternate with prepositionless NP's preceding the direct object.

(3-64)   He mentioned my name to John.

(3-65)   *He mentioned John my name.

(3-66)   John opened the door for Alice.

(3-67)   *John opened Alice the door.

There are even verbs for which some noun phrases can be in either
position and others cannot.

(3-68)   I brought a glass of water to John.

(3-69)   I brought John a glass of water.

(3-70)   I brought a glass of water to the table.

(3-71)   *I brought the table a glass of water.

(3-72)   I bought a new table for Mary.

(3-73)   I bought Mary a new table.

(3-74)   I bought a new table for the dining room.

(3-75)   *I bought the dining room a new table.

In the cases exemplified by the sentences above, it is always
animate nouns which allow preposition deletion and inanimate ones which
do not; this provides added motivation for considering the "to NP" and
"for NP" basic and the prepositionless form derived. It is not entirely
clear whether the restriction that only with animate nouns can the
preposition be deleted applies to all indirect object verbs or only to
some. There appear to be a few instances of prepositionless inanimate
noun phrases:

(3-76)   He gave the house a new coat of paint.

(3-77)   He gave the problem his full attention.

(3-78)   He allowed his imagination full play.

(3-79)   The new carpet lent the room a false air of elegance.

Such examples are relatively rare;[8] only the verb "give" is at all

productive in such forms, and sentence (3-78) might best be explained by

considering "imagination" animate. The only clear thing about (3-79) is

that the "lend" there is not the usual "lend", since the direct objects

of the former are restricted to "air", "aura", and their synonyms,

whereas the direct objects of "lend" with animate subject and animate

indirect object are generally concrete nouns. In many instances with

"give", the direct object is a verbal derivative:

(3-80)   He gave the door a hearty shove.

(3-81)   He gave the rope a sudden tug.

Such constructions are similar to constructions with only a deverbal

direct object, as "take a walk", "do a dance", which should probably be

considered to have an inserted dummy verb, and it is possible that a

similar analysis would give the best description of the cases in which

"give" has an inanimate indirect object.

Even if it can be conclusively argued that only animate noun phrases

permit preposition deletion in an indirect object construction, there

still remains the problem of distinguishing the animate noun phrases

8.   Jespersen (MEG, III, 285) lists nine examples, of which seven use
      the verb "give"; and of those, two are no longer acceptable English
      and two or three are clichés ("give itself the lie", "give imagi-
      nation rein", "if I had given it a thought").

with non-deletable "to" and "for" of sentences (3-64) and (3-66) from the regular indirect objects. Verbs with deletable "for" do at least seem to form two natural semantic classes, although there do not seem to be any other syntactic properties which correlate with the deletability of "for". The two semantic classes are verbs of procuring (procure, get, find, buy, furnish) and verbs of constructing (make, build, sew, draw, ...). The deletability of "to", however, does not even seem to have any semantic regularity. The following pairs of sentences contain semantically similar verbs which differ as to the deletability of "to":

(3-82)   He told John a tale of all his troubles.

(3-83)   *He related John a tale of all his troubles.

(3-84)   She showed him her latest discovery.

(3-85)   *She revealed him her latest discovery.

(3-86)   Mr. Smith mailed her a letter.

(3-87)   *Mr. Smith addressed her a letter.

3.26

Since the deletability of "to" and "for" before animate noun phrases is not predictable from any independently determined syntactic feature of the verb, it follows that this property must be part of the lexical entry for all verbs which take both a direct object and a "to-" or "for-" phrase. A verb such as "tell" will have among its syntactic features something like the following:

(i)   the <u>strict subcategorization feature</u> of occurring in the

frame:____ to NP   NP

(ii)   the <u>selectional features</u> of requiring an animate subject,

an animate noun in the "to NP" phrase, and an abstract direct object

(iii) the <u>operational feature</u> of permitting application of the

rule TIOPREPDEL, (unless a convention is made by which only verbs

which do not permit a given rule to apply are so marked, in which

case <u>relate</u> would be marked as not permitting TIOPREPDEL)

3.27

A few brief remarks should be made about a number of consider-

ations not mentioned above.

3.271

There are apparent indirect objects whose preposition must be

deleted, as in:

(3-88)   He saved me a great deal of trouble.

(3-89)   He spared her much suffering.

These forms are far scarcer than those whose prepositions cannot be

deleted, so instead of an additional phrase structure expansion of VP

into V NP NP just for these cases, the best solution would seem to be to

introduce these indirect objects in the same way as the others (although

which preposition should be used is not clear) and include as an oper-

ational feature of the verbs in question an indication that TIOPREPDEL

is obligatory for them.

3.272

Some indirect objects should be derived from phrases with underlying prepositions other than "to" or "for".

(3-90)   He bore me a grudge.

(3-91)   *He bore a grudge to (for) me.

(3-92)   He bore a grudge against me.

(3-93)   He bore no ill will toward anyone.

These cases are isolated and apparently unsystematic, and will not be considered further.

3.273

There appears to be a systematic relation between some of the indirect objects with "to" and "adverbs of direction" with "to" (cf. sentences (3-68) - (3-71) above); discussion of this relation will be deferred to §3.331.

3.274

There is no good reason for assuming that "to-" and "for-" phrases which occur in the absence of a direct object are introduced any differently than those traditionally called indirect objects. The fact that they do not alternate with a prepositionless form, as in the following examples,

(3-94)   John spoke to the clerk.

(3-95)   *John spoke the clerk.

can be accounted for simply by the fact that they do not meet the structural description for TIOPREPDEL. Therefore the phrase structure rule given in §3.242 should be changed to:

$$\text{VP} \longrightarrow \text{V (with NP)} \quad (\left\{\begin{matrix} \text{to} \\ \text{for} \end{matrix}\right\} \text{NP}) \quad (\text{NP})$$

3.3 Locative and Directional Phrases

The following sentences contain what will be referred to below as "locative" and "directional" phrases:

(3-96)   John sat on the sofa. (locative)

(3-97)   John kept his car in the garage. (locative)

(3-98)   John stepped onto the ice. (directional)

(3-99)   John drove his car into the garage. (directional)

Both these phrase types have been regarded traditionally as adverbs, but Lees[9] includes those in (3-96) and (3-98) as constituents of V_{in} and that in (3-99) as a constituent of V_t; in his analysis, the locative phrase in (3-97) is transformationally derived from a complement construction and is thus derivatively a constituent of V_{tr}, which is one category higher than V_t, and parallel to V_{in}.

In this section, reasons are given for distinguishing locative and directional phrases within the verb phrase construction from locative phrases which are modifiers for the whole verb phrase (§3.31); then follows an argument concerning the best way to introduce such phrases, whether in the phrase structure or by transformation (§3.32). Finally, the relation between locative and directional phrases is examined (§3.33).

3.31 Their place in the verb phrase

Before the question of whether these locative and directional phrases are introduced in the same minimal S as the verb with which they

---

9.   Lees, GEN, pp. 9-11.

are found is discussed, some justification must be given for treating them in a chapter concerned mainly with objects when they have been traditionally regarded simply as adverbs. It is not necessary to go into detail on the difference between sentence adverbs (e.g. "probably"), verb phrase adverbs (e.g. "yesterday"), and constituents on the same level as objects in the base structure (whether they are also called adverbs or not is not of significance) to make it apparent that there is a difference of structure in the two following examples:

(3-100)   John keeps his car in the garage.

(3-101)   John washes his car in the garage.

One indication of this difference is provided by conjunction:

(3-102)   John washes and polishes his car in the garage.

(3-103)   *John washes and keeps his car in the garage.

That the locative in (3-100) is more like an object in structural closeness to the verb than that in (3-101) is seen from the fact that the presence of the locative in (3-100) affects the selection of the verb, while that in (3-101) does not. That is, although it is difficult to find verbs which, considered as phonological entities,[10] actually require the presence of a locative phrase, it is not difficult if one considers a particular semantic reading of a particular verb as the relevant entity. Then in addition to "keep", verbs which require a locative[11] on at least one semantic reading include "leave", "find",

---

10. E.S. Klima has suggested that "dwell" is one such verb.

11. There are actually other constituents which can be used as well as locative phrases with all these verbs, even on the relevant readings. These are discussed below.

"put", "lay", "set", and "stand".

The directional phrase is invariably closely connected to the verb; verbs are classifiable as to whether they permit directional phrases or not, and directional phrases can never be simply tacked on to otherwise complete sentences, as locative phrases sometimes can be. A complete sentence may be followed by a request for further information of the form

(3-104)   Where did that happen?

or

(3-105)   Where did he do that?

but not

(3-106)   *Where did that happen to?

nor

(3-107)   *Where did he do that to?   (*Whither did he do that?)

Thus directional phrases are all parallel to the locative phrase in sentence (3-100), never to that of sentence (3-101). In the remainder of the chapter, locatives of the type in sentence (3-101) will be ignored.

3.32   Phrase structural versus transformational derivation

The two main questions which must be settled in order to determine more specifically the underlying structure of locative and directional phrases in the verb phrase are:

(i)   Are all locative and directional phrases expanded directly in the phrase structure, or are some (or all) of them introduced trans-formationally via some sort of complement construction?

(ii)   Are locative and directional phrases independent of each other?

The remainder of §3.32 is devoted to question (i); question (ii) is the subject of §3.33.

3.321

One strong argument in favor of at least some locative and directional phrases being transformationally derived from an embedded sentence is the non-occurrence of reflexivization in locatives and accusatives.

(3-108)   He kept the gun beside him.

(3-109)   *He kept the gun beside himself.

(3-110)   He pushed the plate away from him.

(3-111)   *He pushed the plate away from himself.[12]

It would seem that since many of the relevant verbs involve motion or position of the subject, there would be many cases in which no locative or directional phrase containing the subject is possible at all, and in such cases there would be no way to tell whether reflexivization is possible or not.

(3-112)   *I took the gun away from me.

(3-113)   *I took the gun away from myself.

(3-114)   *I stood behind me.

(3-115)   *I stood behind myself.

However, perhaps even these cases can be resolved by sentences such as the following:

(3-116)   *You can't take a gun away from you.

(3-117)   You can't take a gun away from yourself.

---

12.   Sentence (3-111) is possible, but only with contrastive stress.

(3-118) *You can't stand behind you.

(3-119) You can't stand behind yourself.

But these examples are not altogether conclusive, since there is neces-

sarily some contrastive emphasis on the final pronoun.

A few intransitive verbs can have a locative phrase containing the

subject even in a simple affirmative sentence. These, like (3-119), show

reflexivization, in contrast to the transitive verbs with locative phrases,

like (3-108). In these examples the meaning is figurative rather than

literal.

(3-120) He was beside himself with anger.

(3-121) He sat by himself.[13]

3.3220

There is particularly strong evidence for the transformational

origin of locative phrases after transitive verbs such as "keep",

"leave", and "find", which, however, cannot be generalized even to the

case of locative phrases after certain other transitive verbs, including

"set", "stand", "lay", "put", and "lock", much less to locatives after

intransitive verbs or to any directional phrases. Consider the following

sentences (in which "keep" could be replaced by "find" or "leave"):

(3-122) John kept the car beside the house.

(3-123) John kept the car clean.

(3-124) John kept the car running.

---

13. That the meaning of the locative in (3-121) is figurative in spite
    of the existence of similar literal locatives such as "He sat by
    Mary" can be seen by the fact that (3-121) is not an answer to
    "Who did he sit by?" and that it is not at all odd to say, "He
    didn't sit by anyone; he sat by himself."

(3-125)   John kept the car locked.

(3-126)   *John kept the car a hobby.[14]

With the exception of the noun phrase in the excluded sentence

(3-126), it appears that the constituents which can occur on this con-

struction are just those which can occur after "be": locatives, adjec-

tives, -ing forms of verbs, and -en forms of verbs. It is much simpler,

therefore, to describe this construction as resulting via an embedding

transformation from underlying structures of roughly the following form:[15]

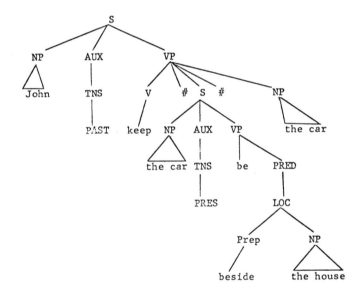

Fig. 3-iii

Underlying structure of (3-122)

---

14. For those who find (3-126) acceptable, the following argument is
     even stronger, since predicate noun phrases are for them not an
     exception to the rule described below.

15. The relative order of the embedded # S # and the direct object
     shown here was established on the basis of TOBJORD; other con-
     siderations may well lead to a reversal of this order.

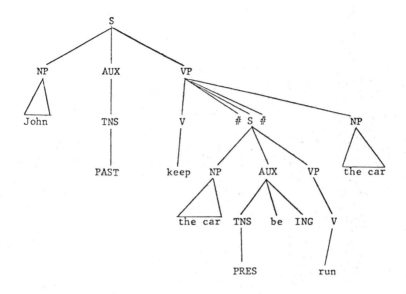

Fig. 3-iv

Underlying structure of (3-124)

It is certainly simpler to exclude predicate noun phrases from partici-
pating in the embedding transformation than to specify independently all
the constituents that can appear after "kept (found, left) NP". The
transformation can be stated as follows[16]:

TBECOMP (obligatory)

$$X - \begin{bmatrix} V \\ +\text{becomp} \end{bmatrix} - Y - \# - NP - PRES - be - (\begin{Bmatrix} EN \\ ING \end{Bmatrix}) - \begin{Bmatrix} VP \\ PRED \end{Bmatrix} - \# - NP - Z$$

$$1 \quad\quad 2 \quad\quad 3 \quad 4 \quad 5 \quad\quad 6 \quad\quad 7 \quad\quad\quad 8 \quad\quad\quad 9 \quad\quad 10 \quad 11 \quad 12$$

$$\Longrightarrow 1\text{-}2\text{-}3\text{-}\emptyset\text{-}\emptyset\text{-}\emptyset\text{-}\emptyset\text{-}8\text{-}9\text{-}\emptyset\text{-}11\text{-}12$$

Conditions: 9 is not analyzable as NP; 11 = 5

3.3221

However, it certainly does not follow from the fact that loca-tives with this class of verbs are transformationally derived that all locative and directional phrases are. The verbs "set", "stand", and "lay", for instance, pose a number of problems in this regard. About the only constituents other than locatives which can follow their direct objects are a few adjectives such as "straight", "upright", or "flat". The constraints are identical with those on intransitive "sit", "stand", and "lie" when the latter have an inanimate subject, but do not overlap completely if the intransitive subject is animate.

(3-127)   The rug lay flat.

(3-128)   John laid the rug flat.

(3-129)   The little boy sat still.

(3-130)   *John set the little boy still.

The intransitive member of each pair, when the subject is inanimate, seems to be related to the transitive member in the same way that intran-sitive and transitive "break" are related (see §2.3), which suggests that the transitive member is fundamental and the intransitive one derived. The contention that the pairs are transformationally related is supported by the fact that many speakers do not distinguish "sit-set" and "lie-lay" morphologically. But some sentences containing the intransitive member with an animate subject, such as (3-129), cannot be so derived, because their sources, such as (3-130), are missing. If those sentences are treated as fundamental in their own right, then very different under- lying structures will be assigned to the following superficially very similar sentences:

(3-131)   The flagpole stood in the corner.

(3-132)   The boy stood in the corner.

Sentence (3-131) is transformationally derived (by TSUBJ) from

(3-133)   "stood the flagpole in the corner",

the subjectless counterpart of

(3-134)   John stood the flagpole in the corner,

so the fact that sentences (3-131) and (3-132) have identical restrictions on the locatives (and the few adjectives) that can occur is not an argu- ment in favor of deriving the locative phrase in (3-132) by embedding. It is not an argument against embedding, either, however, so independent evidence is required. Such evidence is furnished by the following sen- tences:

(3-135)   John stood the flagpole near him.

(3-136)   *John stood the flagpole near himself.

(3-137)   John laid the quilt under him.

(3-138)   *John laid the quilt under himself.

It appears, then, that these locative phrases are also derived from embedded kernels, although by a different transformation than that associated with verbs like "keep". There is therefore no reason to include locative phrases in the phrase structure expansion of verb phrases containing any transitive verbs.

The transformation needed with verbs such as "stand" can be stated as follows:

TLOCCOMP (obligatory)

$$\text{NP - AUX -} \begin{bmatrix} \text{V} \\ \text{+loccomp} \end{bmatrix} \text{- X - \# - NP - TNS - be - LOC - \# - (NP) - Y}$$

$$\quad 1 \quad\quad 2 \quad\quad\quad\quad 3 \quad\quad\quad\quad 4 \quad\ 5 \quad 6 \quad\ 7 \quad\ 8 \quad\ 9 \quad\ 10 \quad\ 11 \quad\ 12$$

$$\Longrightarrow \quad 1\text{-}2\text{-}3\text{-}4\text{-}\emptyset\text{-}\emptyset\text{-}\emptyset\text{-}\emptyset\text{-}9\text{-}\emptyset\text{-}11\text{-}12$$

Condition:[17] Either $1 = 6$ and $11 = \emptyset$, or $11 = 6$

3.323

Among the verbs which take directional phrases, "go" seems intuitively the simplest. That "go" is syntactically fundamental as well is suggested by the following examples:

(3-139) Mary drove Bill crazy.

(3-140) *Mary drove Bill sad.

(3-141) Bill went crazy.

(3-142) *Bill went sad.

Note also that the first of the following two sentences is ambiguous, but the second is not.

(3-143) John sent Bill to his sister's house;

(3-144) John sent Bill to his death.

---

17. The first clause in the condition corresponds to the case of "The flagpole stood in the corner", the second to "John stood the flagpole in the corner".

The difference can be accounted for by considering the possibilities
with "go":

(3-145)   Bill went to his (=Bill's) sister's house.

(3-146)   Bill went to John's sister's house.

(3-147)   Bill went to his (=Bill's) death.

(3-148)   *Bill went to John's death.

In general, any constituent which can appear in place of a directional phrase (e.g. "crazy" in (3-139)) with a verb which normally requires
a directional phrase can also appear with "go", and many apparent irregu-
larities in directional phrases, such as the lack of ambiguity of (3-144),
can be resolved by considering there to be an underlying "go". But
unfortunately, simply postulating an underlying embedded sentence containing "go" with all verbs which take directional phrases does not
account correctly for all the actual possible and impossible sentences.
For instance, if it is assumed that (3-144) contains (3-147) as an
embedded sentence, there is no reason why (3-141) could not be similarly
embedded to give

(3-149)   *John sent Bill crazy.

It is also not clear why one but not the other of the following sentences
should be possible if an underlying "go" is the only relevant factor; it
may be that there is more than one "go".

(3-150)   John drove Bill and Mary together.

(3-151)   *John drove Bill and Mary steady.

However, it seems that out of all these pieces of evidence, the ones
that carry most weight for the question at hand are the non-ambiguity

example ((3-143) - (3-148)) and the lack of reflexivization mentioned
earlier ((3-110) - (3-111)), since it appears that the other phenomena
have to be treated as exceptional independently of whether directional
phrases are considered to be derived by embedding or not. The conclusion
from the main evidence is that at least some directional phrases after
transitive verbs are derived from embedded sentences containing "go" by
a transformation of the following form:

TGOCOMP (obligatory)

$$X - \begin{bmatrix} V \\ +gocomp \end{bmatrix} - Y - \# - NP - TNS - go - Z - \# - NP - W$$

1   2   3   4   5   6   7   8   9   10   11

$\Longrightarrow$ 1-2-3-Ø-Ø-Ø-Ø-8-Ø-10-11

Condition: 10 = 5

The examples given so far do not apply to intransitive verbs
followed by directional phrases, such as:

(3-152)   The swallows flew to Capistrano.

None of the non-directional constituents which sometimes follow "go" can
replace the directional phrase after other intransitive verbs, so even
that marginal argument for transformational derivation is lacking for the
intransitive verbs. Since it would complicate the embedding transformation (by requiring a disjunctive condition like that of TLOCCOMP) to
derive these directional phrases by embedding and would not result in
any simplification of the phrase structure, it is simpler to let all of
the directional phrases following intransitive verbs be introduced and
expanded directly in the phrase structure, and derive only those following

transitive verbs by embedding sentences containing "go", with a few special restrictions (not given here) on the embedding transformation to deal with the anomalies mentioned above.

3.33 The relation between locative and directional phrases

Independent of the question of transformational versus phrase structure origin of locative and directional phrases, there is the question of whether the two kinds of phrase are related or not. Consider the following sentence:

(3-153)   She took him into the store and left him there.

"There" is clearly a Pro-form, but it is not immediately obvious how it is introduced in such a position. The repeated element is apparent in the following sentences:

(3-154)   Mary went to the store in the morning and Bill went
          there later.

(3-155)   Mary was born in that house and died there too.

But underlying (3-153) cannot be a sentence with the directional phrase repeated, since "leave" cannot be followed by a directional phrase.

(3-156)   *She took him into the store and left him into the store.

The occurrence of "there" in (3-153) is really replacing "in the store", so that the Pro constituent is a locative phrase; but then by the general principle that Pro-forms are always repeated forms, there must be a locative phrase earlier in that sentence, and in particular, it must be contained in "into the store". Considering the various prepositions which can be used with locative and directional phrases, one finds that there are rather natural pairs,[18] many of which are identical pairs, such

---

18. The extensiveness of the list of such pairs was brought to my
     attention by Jeffrey Gruber, whose doctoral dissertation (MIT,
     forthcoming) contains semantic arguments for considering the
     relation between the two sets a regular one.

as the following:

Locative	Directional
in	in(to)
on	on(to)
near	near (to)
beside	alongside
across	across
at	to

The most natural way to account for these facts would appear to be with a phrase structure rule which expands directional phrases as follows:

$$DIR \longrightarrow to \ LOC$$

and rules such as

$$\begin{array}{cc} to & - \ in \\ 1 & 2 \end{array} \Longrightarrow \emptyset \ - \ 2 + 1$$

$$\begin{array}{cc} to & - \ across \\ 1 & 2 \end{array} \Longrightarrow \emptyset \ - \ 2$$

$$\begin{array}{cc} to & - \ at \\ 1 & 2 \end{array} \Longrightarrow 1 \ - \ \emptyset^{19}$$

However, since directional and locative phrases never occur in the same kernel verb phrase, there is no reason not to simply introduce them together in the phrase structure at the same place in the expansion of VP, as .... (to) LOC ..., and dispense with the additional nonterminal symbol DIR entirely.[20] For the full rule, see the end of §3.331.

---

19. It would appear that the derived constituent structure is rather different in this example than in the two preceding ones. However, these rules are preceded by TACCPREP, which puts the two prepositions in parallel structure; see §3.331.

20. If it becomes necessary to differentiate directional from locative phrases by more complicated means than the presence or absence of the preposition "to", then where the rule in §3.331 has "(to) LOC", there would simply be instead $\left\{ \begin{array}{c} DIR \\ LOC \end{array} \right\}$, and DIR would then be expanded into "to LOC" and whatever other expansions are required.

3.331

In §3.283 it was mentioned that there seems to be some systematic connection between some indirect objects with "to" and some directional phrases. The following verbs, for instance, can have either an
indirect object with "to" or a directional phrase, but not both at once:
"carry", "take", "return", "throw", "bring", "fling", "send", and "pour".

(3-157)   John sent the package to Chicago.

(3-158)   John sent the package to Mr. Simms.

(3-159)   *John sent the package to Mr. Simms to Chicago.

(3-160)   *John sent the package to Chicago to Mr. Simms.

This complementary distribution would suggest that indirect objects and
directional phrases are really two forms of the same constituent; if
true, this would conflict with the claim that indirect objects are part
of the kernel verb phrase structure while directional phrases with
transitive verbs are derived by embedding. However, many verbs which
can take an indirect object with "to" cannot take a directional phrase,
and conversely. Among those which can take only an indirect object are
"give", "feed", "offer", "pay", "promise", "owe", "tell", "read",
"teach", and "show"; among those which can take only a directional
phrase are "drive", "chase", "lead", and "seduce".

It might be suggested that the lack of complete overlapping between
the two kinds of constituents is due simply to selectional restrictions
between the verb and the items within the indirect object - directional
constituent if both should be generated in the phrase structure; in
particular, it might appear at first that if the noun phrase in that

constituent must be human, then there can be only an indirect object, and if it cannot be human, there can be only a directional phrase. However, such a proposal overlooks two relevant facts: first, that there are verbs which can have among their directional phrases one of the form "to + NP" where the NP is human and which nevertheless cannot have an indirect object:

(3-161)   The soldiers led the captured prisoners to the King.

(3-162)   *The soldiers led the King the captured prisoners.

and second, those verbs which can have only an indirect object cannot have all the prepositions that the accusative phrases can have.

(3-163)   *The farmer fed some hay away from the cows.

Greater success in expressing all the constraints mentioned so far might be achieved by introducing complements and indirect object phrases at the same point in the expansion of VP (to indicate that they never both occur) but leaving their structure differentiated from the start. Before the rules are formalized, it should be pointed out that introducing complements and indirect objects together captures the fact that not only directional phrases and indirect objects cannot appear together, but neither can locative and directional phrases, nor locatives and indirect objects.[21]

These constraints are all expressed in the following rules, which supersede the rules of §3.274 and §2.3.

---

21.   There are seeming counterexamples to the last remark; e.g., "John sent a postcard to his aunt in Lexington." But there is no sentence "*John sent his aunt a postcard in Lexington;" there is rather "John sent his aunt in Lexington a postcard." Thus the first sentence does not contain a locative with the structure of locatives in (3-100) or (3-108); its locative is a reduced relative clause modifying the indirect object, "his aunt".

$$VP \longrightarrow be \ PRED$$

$$\longrightarrow V \ \text{(with NP)} \ (\left\{ \begin{array}{c} \left\{ \begin{array}{c} to \\ for \end{array} \right\} NP \\ \# \ S \ \# \end{array} \right\}) \ NP$$

$$\longrightarrow V \ \text{(with NP)} \ \text{((to) LOC)}$$

LOC will be expanded as PREPL NP, where PREPL covers the class of prepositions that can be used in locative phrases, and there are selectional constraints between the noun phrase and the preposition ("at the seashore" but "in the city"). Both these prepositions and the ones introduced by name ("with", "to", and "for") are to be represented in terms of features, with one feature which they all share, +Prep. The symbol PREP used in transformational rules is to be understood as an abbreviation for the feature notation $\left[+Prep \right]$.

The transformations discussed so far apply in the following order:

I.   TSUBJ (last form in §2.30)

II.   TIOPREPDEL (§3.242)

III.   TACCPREP:[22] (obligatory)

   to - PREP $\Longrightarrow$ $\emptyset$ - 1 ⟨ 2
   1   2

IV.   TBECOMP (§3.3220)

V.   TLOCCOMP (§3.3221)

VI.   TGOCOMP (§3.323)

VII.   TOBJORD: The form given in §2.30 does not allow for more than one PREP - NP, nor for a PREP - NP preceding NP NP, a situation which can arise when TIOPREPDEL has applied. Provision must also be

22. TACCPREP does not supplant the rules mentioned in §3.33; it is needed here to make the pair of prepositions introducing a directional phrase behave as a single preposition in TOBJORD.

made for interchanging pairs of PREP - NP phrases, since in the actual
sentence, "with NP" should follow "to NP"; but care must be taken so
that the transformation which effects that interchange does not reapply
ad infinitum. In addition, complements which are not of the form
PREP - NP must be moved to the right of the noun phrase. These conditions
can all be met by breaking the transformation into two parts as follows:

VII - 1. <u>TOBJORD-1</u> (cyclical)

X - V - PREP - NP - Y - NP - NP $\implies$ 1-2-$\emptyset$-$\emptyset$-5-6-7+3+4
1   2   3   4   5   6   7

VII - 2. <u>TOBJORD-2</u> (non-cyclical)

X - V - (PREP) - $\left\{ {S \atop NP} \right\}$ - Y - NP - e $\implies$ 1-2-$\emptyset$-$\emptyset$-5-6-3+4
1   2   3   4   5   6   7

A few sample derivations will show how these transformations apply.
Noun phrases are represented in final graphic form, since their internal
structure is not under consideration here.

(3-164) The boy fastened the nut onto the wheel with a wrench.

$\#\#$ - (the boy)$_{NP}$ - (Past)$_{AUX}$ - (fasten)$_V$ - with - (a wrench)$_{NP}$ - $\#$ -
((the nut)$_{NP}$ - (Past)$_{AUX}$ - (go)$_V$ - to - (on)$_{PREPL}$ - (the wheel)$_{NP}$)$_S$ - $\#$
(the nut)$_{NP}$ - $\#\#$

TSUBJ and TIOPREPDEL do not apply

$\implies$ .... (to + on)$_{PREPL}$ ....
TACCPREP

$\implies$ $\#\#$ - the boy - Past - fasten - with a wrench - to+on -
TGOCOMP   the wheel - the nut - $\#\#$

$\overset{\Longrightarrow}{\text{TOBJORD-1}}$ ## - the boy - Past - fasten - to+on the wheel - the nut - with a wrench - ##

$\overset{\Longrightarrow}{\text{TOBJORD-2}}$ ## - the boy - Past - fasten - the nut - to+on - the wheel - with a wrench - ##

(3-165)   He showed Mary the pictures with a projector

- (he)$_{NP}$ - (Past)$_{AUX}$ - (show)$_V$ - with - (a projector)$_{NP}$ - to - (Mary)$_{NP}$ - (the pictures)$_{NP}$ -

$\overset{\Longrightarrow}{\text{TIOPREPDEL}}$ ## he Past show with a projector Mary the pictures ##

$\overset{\Longrightarrow}{\text{TOBJORD-1}}$ ## he Past show Mary the pictures with a projector ##

(3-166)   He climbed onto the roof with a ladder

- (he)$_{NP}$ - (Past)$_{AUX}$ - (climb)$_V$ - with - (a ladder)$_{NP}$ - to - (on)$_{PREPL}$ - (the roof)$_{NP}$ -

TSUBJ, TIOPREPDEL do not apply

$\overset{\Longrightarrow}{\text{TACCPREP}}$ .... (to+on)$_{PREPL}$ ....

TOBJORD-1 does not apply

$\overset{\Longrightarrow}{\text{TOBJORD-2}}$ ## he Past climb to+on the roof with a ladder ##

TOBJORD-2 is not permitted to reapply because it is marked non-cyclical.

(3-167)   The prize money bought a new coat for Mary

- (Past)$_{AUX}$ - (buy)$_V$ - with - (the prize money)$_{NP}$ - for - (Mary)$_{NP}$ - (a new coat)$_{NP}$ -

$\xrightarrow{\text{TSUBJ}}$ ## the prize money Past buy for Mary a new coat ##

TIOPREPDEL could apply, giving "The prize money bought Mary a new coat";
if it is not applied, the next transformation which applies is TOBJORD-2:

$\xrightarrow{\text{TOBJORD-2}}$ ## the prize money Past buy a new coat for Mary ##

3.4 Derived Direct Object

In §3.1 it was suggested that the direct object relation might be
defined as (NP, VP) in case all other noun phrases dominated by VP are
dominated by some other node below VP as well. The rules given in
§3.331 have other instances of NP also dominated directly by VP, namely
indirect objects and the NP's in with-phrases. However, none of the rules
would be affected if intermediate nodes such as "INSTR" (for instrumental
with-phrases) and "IO" (for indirect object to- and for-phrases) were
added, so the rules in §3.1 are not a strong argument against the possibility of defining direct object as (NP, VP). Considering only the rules
given there, it is slightly more economical not to introduce the extra
intermediate nodes, but it is not at all unlikely that further considerations will show some reasons for having such nodes.

Since no strong evidence either for or against the suggested definition of underlying direct object has been presented, there is less
basis for suggesting and comparing definitions of derived direct object
than there was in the case of the subject relation. Therefore the following discussion of various possible derived direct objects is essentially informal and is concerned mainly with suggesting derived con-

structions which resemble direct objects in various ways, without coming to any conclusions about which ones should actually count as derived direct objects.

3.41 Indirect objects

One constituent already considered which shares at least one property of direct objects is the indirect object in its prepositionless form. Whereas the indirect object with its preposition cannot be the subject of a passive sentence, the prepositionless form can:

(3-168) *Mary was given a book to by John.

(3-169) Mary was given a book by John.

The prepositionless indirect object does not, however, share with the direct object the ability to form a nominalization with "of":

(3-170) the giving of 30 acres of land to the college

(3-171) *the giving of the college of 30 acres of land

3.42 Objectivized locative phrases

There is a class of derived constructions which does share both the above-mentioned properties of direct objects. The following pairs of sentences are clearly related:

(3-172) John smeared paint on the wall.

(3-173) John smeared the wall with paint.

(3-174) John planted peas and corn in his garden.

(3-175) John planted his garden with peas and corn.

(3-176) John rubbed butter on the burn.

(3-177) John rubbed the burn with butter.

The first sentence of each pair is derived by TLOCCOMP and TOBJORD-2.
Since the existence of a sentence of the second type depends only on the
main verb in the sentence and the preposition used in the locative
phrase, the most natural derivation of (3-173), (3-175), and (3-177)
would be from (3-172), (3-174), and (3-176) respectively, by another
transformation. The verbs which permit this transformation must be
marked for it, although only verbs which permit locative complements
need be so marked, since constructions with other verbs automatically
fail to satisfy the structural description of the transformation. The
required preposition is whatever preposition carries the least information in connection with the given verb and the object of the preposition, although it is not clear exactly how such a requirement is to
be formulated. There are many cases in which such neutral prepositions
will have to be specified, in addition to the constructions under consideration, as for example in simple sentences specifying residence:

   (3-178)   John lives in (*on, *at) Apartment 36.

   (3-179)   John lives on (*in, *at) the third floor.

   (3-180)   John lives at (*in, *on) 47 Winchester Street.

Even when more than one preposition is possible, only one is neutral,
or semantically empty; "near" could be used in any of the three sentences
above, but only the given prepositions allow the sentences to be paraphrased without any preposition in the following way:

   (3-181)   Apartment 36 is where John lives.

   (3-182)   The third floor is where John lives.

   (3-183)   47 Winchester Street is where John lives.

One way to treat this problem is to include among the choices of expansions for PREPL, the preposition which occurs in locative phrases, one dummy preposition which is not realized until after its object and the verb are selected. The details of the selection will not be gone into here; such a preposition will be referred to as PREPLDUM.

The transformation which accounts for the derivation of sentences (3-173), (3-175), and (3-177) puts the object of a dummy preposition in a locative phrase into object position, and postposes "with" plus the original object:

VIII. TOBJLOC (optional)

$$X - \begin{bmatrix} V \\ +objloc \end{bmatrix} - NP - PREPLDUM - NP \implies 1\text{-}2\text{-}5\text{+}with\text{+}3\text{-}\emptyset\text{-}\emptyset$$
$$1 \qquad 2 \qquad\quad 3 \qquad 4 \qquad\quad 5$$

The resulting derived object can be made the subject of a passive.

(3-184)   The wall was smeared with paint by the naughty boys.

(3-185)   The slice of bread was spread with fresh butter.

It can also be used in an of-phrase in a nominalization:

(3-186)   the smearing of the wall with paint

3.421

Other cases of derived objects in which the original object appears in a with-phrase come from "to NP" and "for NP" phrases which do not behave as indirect objects.

(3-187)   I entrusted my money to him.

(3-188)   I entrusted him with my money.

(3-189)   He provided shelter for the children.

(3-190)   He provided the children with shelter.

In some constructions, the original object appears in an of-phrase rather than a with-phrase:

(3-191)   He emptied the water from the milk bottle.

(3-192)   He emptied the milk bottle of water.

3.422

It might be suggested that the simplest way to derive sentences such as (3-172) and (3-173) would be to postulate an underlying form containing both prepositions and set up a transformation which allows deletion of either preposition, moving the prepositionless NP next to the verb if it is not already there. Sentences (3-172) and (3-173) would then come from something like

(3-193)   John smeared with paint on the wall.

One argument against such an underlying form is that there is a with-phrase already established in underlying forms, and it can co-occur with the with-phrases of sentences (3-173), (3-175), etc.:

(3-194)   John spread the bread with butter with a penknife.

The two with-phrases are certainly not alike:

(3-195)   John spread butter on the bread with a penknife.

(3-196)   *John spread a penknife on the bread with butter.

3.43 Of-phrases

Considering the number of prepositional phrases which occur in the verb phrase and the variety of derived direct objects, it might be suggested that what has been called the underlying direct object is itself derived from a prepositional phrase, so that the verb phrase contains nothing but the verb, zero or more prepositional phrases, and possibly an embedded # S #. The most likely preposition would seem to be "of", since (a) most adjectives which take objects have "of": "proud of", "afraid of", "aware of", etc., and (b) "of" occurs before the direct object in nominalizations.

However, there are two independent strong arguments against such a view. One stems from nominalizations such as (3-186) and

(3-197)   the emptying of the bucket of its water.

That is, clause (b) of the preceding paragraph is not a valid reason for postulating an underlying "of" with direct objects, because derived objects can also take "of" in nominalizations. Furthermore, there are reasons for postulating underlying of-phrases which do not result in direct objects. Consider the following sentences:

(3-198)   They accused John of perjury.

(3-199)   The thief stripped John of all his valuables.

If "accuse of", "strip of", and "persuade of" were taken to be single verbs, then a new construction "V NP NP" would have to be established together with a transformation to correctly place the "of". Even if a "V NP NP" construction is set up for the exceptional verbs "envy" and "forgive", these latter do not behave in the same way as the verbs with "of".

(3-200)   the crime he was convicted of

(3-201)   the jewels she was robbed of·

(3-202)   *his beauty he was envied

(3-203)   *the sins he was forgiven

The suggestion that the of-phrases in (3-198) - (3-201) are
transformationally introduced also fails, because there are no simpler
sentences with the same selectional restrictions from which these might
be derived.

It being determined that there must be an underlying of-phrase,
there remains the question of its order among the constituents. A
sentence such as

(3-204)   John persuaded him of the truth of our claim with a
          devious argument.

can be derived using TOBJORD-1 and TOBJORD-2 if the order of the underlying constituents is

with NP - of NP - NP.

Similarly,

(3-205)   He talked to John of philosophy.

can be derived using the same two transformations if the underlying
order is

of NP - to NP - NP.

The revised expansion of VP is:

$$
VP \longrightarrow \left\{ \begin{array}{l} \text{be PRED} \\[2ex] V \text{ (with NP)} \text{ (of NP)} \left(\left\{ \begin{array}{l} \left\{ \begin{array}{l} \text{to} \\ \text{for} \end{array} \right\} \text{NP} \\[1ex] \# \ \text{S} \ \# \end{array} \right\} \right) \text{NP} \\[4ex] V \text{ (with NP)} \text{ (of NP)} \left(\left\{ \begin{array}{l} \text{(to) LOC} \\ \left\{ \begin{array}{l} \text{to} \\ \text{for} \end{array} \right\} \text{NP} \end{array} \right\} \right) \end{array} \right\}
$$

Not only do these underlying of-phrases not become direct objects, but they do not even share with direct objects the property of taking "of" in an -ing nominalization:

 (3-206) Some people complain of injustices.

 (3-207) The walrus talked of cabbages and kings.

 (3-208) *The complaining of injustices is strictly forbidden.

 (3-209) *The talking of cabbages and kings is strictly forbidden.

The last two non-sentences contrast with nominalizations of sentences with an underlying direct object:

 (3-210) The entering of houses is strictly forbidden.

3.5 Concluding Remarks

The phrase structure expansion of VP given in §3.42 is not by any means complete, and the transformations given in §3.331 and §3.410 do not exhaust the description of even those constituents included in the given expansion of VP. Complement constructions have not been treated at all except where there was a question of whether or not a certain constituent was introduced by embedding or not.[23] Clausal objects, whose description raises a number of interesting problems, have been totally ignored. Among the other verb phrase constructions which have been omitted from consideration are reciprocals, cognate objects, causatives, and inserted dummy verbs.

---

23. A detailed treatment of complements can be found in the doctoral dissertation of Peter S. Rosenbaum, M.I.T., 1965.

The emphasis has been on establishing the underlying structure of the verb phrase in certain cases where there might be reason to suspect that the underlying form differs more or less radically from the super- ficial structure. Some attention has also been paid to the notion of derived direct object, and the suggestion that direct objects are derived from prepositional phrases has been examined and rejected.

BIBLIOGRAPHY

Chomsky, Noam A.   The logical structure of Linguistic Theory.
Cambridge: The M.I.T. Library, 1955.

Syntactic Structures. The Hague: Mouton & Co., 1957.

"A transformational approach to syntax". In
A.A. Hill (ed.), Proceedings of the Third Texas
Conference on Problems of Linguistic Analysis in
English, 1958. Austin: The University of Texas,
1962. Reprinted in J.A. Fodor and J.J. Katz,
The Structure of Language; Readings in the Philosophy
of Language. Englewood Cliffs: Prentice-Hall, Inc.,
1964, pp. 155-210.

"Current issues in linguistic theory", in J.A. Fodor
and J.J. Katz, The Structure of Language; Readings
in the Philosophy of Language. Englewood Cliffs:
Prentice-Hall, Inc., 1964, pp. 50-118.

Aspects of the Theory of Syntax. Cambridge: The
M.I.T. Press, forthcoming.

Curme, George O.   Syntax, Vol. III of Hans Kurath and G.O. Curme,
A Grammar of the English Language. 3 vols., Boston:
D.C. Heath & Co., 1931.

Fillmore, C.J.   Indirect Object Constructions in English and the
Ordering of Transformations. Columbus: Ohio State
University, Project on Syntactic Analysis, Report
No. 1, 1962.

Jespersen, Otto   A Modern English Grammar on Historical Principles. 7 vols.,
London: George Allen & Unwin, Ltd., 1909-1949.

The Philosophy of Grammar. London: George Allen &
Unwin, Ltd., 1924.

Katz, Jerrold J. and
Postal, Paul M.   An Integrated Theory of Linguistic Descriptions.
Cambridge: The M.I.T. Press, 1964.

Lees, Robert B.   "The grammar of English nominalizations",
                       International Journal of American Linguistics.
                       Bloomington: Publication Twelve of the Indiana
                       University Research Center in Anthropology,
                       Folklore, and Linguistics, 1960.

Long, Ralph B.   The Sentence and Its Parts: A Grammar of Contempo-
                       rary English. Chicago: University of Chicago
                       Press, 1961.

Paul, Hermann.   Principles of the History of Language. trans.
                       H.A. Strong. London: Swan Sonnenschein, Lowrey,
                       and Co., 1888.

Postal, Paul.   "Constituent structure", International Journal of
                       American Linguistics. Bloomington: Publication
                       Thirty of the Indiana University Research Center
                       in Anthropology, Folklore, and Linguistics, 1964.

Steinthal, H.   Charakteristik der Hauptsächlichen Typen des
                       Sprachbaues. Berlin: 1860.

425 P37s 1979

DATE DUE			